Auras and Colours

A Guide to Working with Subtle Energies

Paul Lambillion

Gateway

Gateway
an imprint of
Gill & Macmillan Ltd
Hume Avenue
Park West
Dublin 12
with associated companies throughout the world
www.gillmacmillan.ie

© 2001 Paul Lambillion
0 7171 3232 3
Index compiled by John Loftus
Print origination by Alanna Corballis
Printed by ColourBooks Ltd, Dublin

The paper used in this book is made from
the wood pulp of managed forests.
For every tree felled, at least one tree is planted,
thereby renewing natural resources.

A catalogue record is available for this book
from the British Library.

7 9 10 8 6

Dedication

To my family, friends
and all those who have supported me
and my work over the years.

Thank you.

Paul

CONTENTS

Contents

INTRODUCTION

To be alive on the planet today is, at one and the same time, an exhilarating, yet puzzling, experience.

That life is changing with an increasing rapidity is evident to even the most isolated and blinkered of human souls. For an ever growing number of us, the changes we encounter can best be understood as a heightening of our perceptual abilities and sensitivities. Our capacity to influence and change the events and circumstances in our lives, rather than view them as purely external, almost random, series of accidents that happen to us, also seems to be expanding. We no longer want to accept what we are told to do or think. We wish to think for ourselves.

The search to understand and obtain a glimpse of the hidden side of life is becoming more prevalent. In society as a whole, there is a feeling that we have all been duped, that something has been kept from us, as if we are deemed somehow unworthy of knowing more, beyond the limits of an apparently hostile three-dimensional world. Philosophies and religions have often tended to support this concept of unworthiness, denying in us any kind of specialness or divinity of our own; following a particular creed or dogma usually means we are required to hand over responsibility for ourselves and thus our power to change and grow.

But eventually we learn that there are not really any three-dimensional solutions to three-dimensional problems. The answer and the truth lie elsewhere, behind what we see and the search to know and see the bigger picture gains pace.

There are a great many books and writings on esoteric subjects that were hitherto the province of the few. I have no wish to duplicate this work, nor to confuse those already searching for an understanding of the four-, five- and six-dimensional worlds and beyond. This is neither an additional New Age text-book, nor another 'life story' to affirm my supposed unique gifts and abilities. Rather, it is a personal appreciation of the under-standing I have gained of the remarkable 'light of the world', the hidden realms, worlds of energies, light, auras and subtle forms, all placed within the framework of my own experiences.

My belief is that we are all special. We can all access far greater awareness and dimensions of possibility within our-selves. What I see, know and experience is the province of every man, woman and child, not just a favoured, gifted few.

Since 1984, I have spent my time as a full-time healer, coun-sellor, visionary and teacher. I am fortunate and privileged in that I am consulted in my work, both in the UK and overseas, by thousands of people, many of whom I can help at least a lit-tle. But my teaching and counsel is always given on the under-standing that what I experience, what I can see and do, is equal-ly available and accessible to all.

Many of you will, I hope, recognise the experiences I relate. For some of you, it may help to dispel some of the fear, anxiety and even guilt felt by many who come to see me.

We are all on a journey towards a place of harmony and goodness, somewhere beyond the old conflicting ways. My wife, family and close friends share with me the pains and the joys, the hardships and blessings of my journey — a journey without end. My hope is that this work will serve to assist you as you make your way on your own journey towards a greater awareness.

May love and light and wisdom be yours.

Paul Lambillion
Bury St Edmunds
Suffolk, UK

A PRELUDE

'It won't be easy, life on earth in this time isn't,' the tall figure told me. Not exactly a conversation it seemed, more the under-lining of an agreement.

'You know why you are going. We will do all we can to help you retain memories, and where necessary, to re-awaken.'

The being I was communicating with was one of several, all very bright, incandescent entities whose fluid faces changed and glowed as we were together. I knew them, but I couldn't name them. They were familiar, very familiar, yet strangely without the kind of identity to which I am accustomed.

There was much activity in this bright, beautiful place, a lit-tle reminiscent of an embarkation hall, although somehow more ordered, more peaceful than that.

'Remember us!' the voice boomed, the last words of our dia-logue. They pierced my mind, or what was my mental self whilst there. I knew I wouldn't forget, completely.

Then there was a sudden tugging. A strong, almost magnetic pull.

I entered a space I had seen before — tunnel-like, yet not a tunnel, more cavernous perhaps. I was soon face to face with whom I would be. We'd met before, briefly, in odd moments after the conception of this body and my commitment to come.

Much noise, and then I came into this new place. It was sti-fling and I had to breathe in an unusual way, not the subtle rhythmic pulsing in me as before. A deep, gasping, strangely heavy and torpid experience. I remembered this also. I had done it before.

'Don't let the light fade,' I cried inside. I could see them — the person who was to be my mother for this life and the other one, who held me up in the air and looked me over.

The light was bright here, but did not compare to the vibrancy I had left behind.

Sadly, the real, sparkling light seemed gradually to be fading, with only the heavy, dull forms remaining, easy to perceive in their earthly density.

'Don't let the beautiful light go!' I implored in my heart.

And they didn't. At least, not all of it.

CHAPTER 1
THE FORMATIVE YEARS

Anyone who does not welcome
the Kingdom of God like a child
will never enter it.
Mark 10:15

Life is full of wonder for us as children, even when we are born into difficult circumstances and into an environment that is scarred and neglected through years of chaos.

My formative years in North London following the war were certainly less than lavish but were exciting nonetheless. Even through that time I can recall a sense of optimism and an inner belief that things would improve. Deprivation would disappear and life for us all would take a positive upturn. This was the belief of the working-class family that I was born into, living in a ground-floor apartment in a large house not far from King's Cross.

The surroundings were far from beautiful in any conventional sense, the view from our flat peppered in all directions with the remnants of the Blitz — bomb sites, shrapnel, strange little stubs where iron railings were removed, melted down and used for the war effort, the remaining buildings in poor repair.

My parents did their best for me and my elder sister, in spite of being emotionally scarred and drained by the intensity and duration of the conflict. But there was a prevailing hope around at all times as they sought better housing in one of the new estates being developed in the countryside of Essex and the home counties.

Childhood memories for me mainly centre around one or two types of feeling and experience. Firstly, the highly charged emotionalism in our household and community — a kind of explosive relief that poured into a growing, yet still chaotic, freedom that had been suppressed for six years or so.

There was suppressed anger everywhere.

And then there was the contrast in light. The drab greyness of London, the little garden we shared and then the powerful colours that I could not yet consciously understand. My senses were not yet numbed by an adult consciousness and I remember clearly the sounds and smells of that time — flowers in the garden, the smell of Granny's snuff tin, crowing cockerels in my neighbour's backyard and the rag and bone man calling us to swap rags for china — and the colours that accompanied them.

Early Visions

An early encounter with the hidden side of life, which was not to make any real sense to me until many years later, revolved around our family religion.

My mother was a devout Catholic and attendance at Mass was a must for us as children. I admit, I enjoyed going to Mass, and still do, though I am not sure my reasons were always in accord with the official thinking of the church at the time. I was often viewed as a naughty, precocious child, 'highly strung' and the victim of an overactive imagination. I was always fascinated by what happened around the altar, as the priest chanted in Latin, the consecration of the bread and wine approached and suddenly the whole area at that end of the church would ignite, and become bathed in a beautiful, white and gold light, teeming with silver blue strands. The priest and everyone around him would be surrounded by the most beautiful swirling radiations, and people would appear as if from nowhere, some clearly human, though to me they seemed transparent as I could see through them to the wall behind. Their appearance was ephemeral, ghostlike, and yet real.

Most of these souls would be dressed in ordinary, everyday clothes, but one or two were not and looked to me like angels I had seen in books, only without their wings.

The ceiling of the church would be lined by a mantle of blue-white light and I can remember the tingling in my neck and down my back while observing this wonderful phenomenon. I often had tears in my eyes, the beautiful feelings being so strong.

My mother would fumble her rosary beads, puzzled by my reactions, and kneeling next to me in the pew would give me a knowing glance so as to keep my mind on God and not on whatever it was that distracted me.

Some days, on the pew next to us, and sometimes behind us, an old Irishman would appear. He had a beautiful sparkle in his eyes and would say gently to me, 'Hello little fella,' as I turned to look at him. He was always relaxed, smiling and attentive to what was going on in the Mass without being overly absorbed in it.

One day, the man appeared as he usually did; I never saw him enter or leave the church. He sat down next to me and then, to my horror, somebody else approached where we were sitting, genuflected and crossed themselves, and was about to sit on top of this man. He didn't react, so I protested on his behalf. 'Don't sit on him,' I remember yelling. My embarrassed mother turned and frowned, then apologised as the lady squeezed into the seat next to me and proceeded to sit on the gentleman. He moved at last and stood in the aisle of the church, his image gradually fading from my view.

After the Mass, at home, found me describing to my mother the appearance of the person who I had seen week in, week out at the church.

'Don't be silly,' she said, 'that was old Danny McIlroy, and he's been in Heaven with Jesus for years now.'

Perplexed and shocked by this revelation, my little mind was in turmoil. I accepted, as I must, what I had been told; at my protestations, my mother raised her eyes skywards in despair. But he hadn't looked dead to me. He seemed happy and not at all threatening and continued to appear for some time afterwards.

I suppose I should have seen something strange in the fact that he never put anything in the collection plate when it came around. This was one of many occasions where the 'dead' appeared to me, and I began to recognise them as such. It happens to all children at some time or other. It will have happened to you, but you may have forgotten.

The brilliant lights and colours I saw, especially vivid and clear at emotional high points, have continued to appear and I still enjoy and wonder at them now. Later, I will explain in more detail the meaning behind these wonderful insights into hidden realities and dimensions, the magical worlds we have forgotten and even fear.

An Early Understanding

These early encounters were my first experiences of an awareness I was to understand much more in adulthood. My perceptions of activity around the altar were the manifestations of a natural sensitivity to a vast range of phenomena. I observed with such clarity and excitement the occupants of the fourth and fifth dimensions and the aura of light that envelops all things.

During childhood, we are generally open to such perceptions and visions, but this is often lost as, through adolescence and into adult life, the more logical and sometimes cynical aspects of our consciousness take hold.

My vision in those early years enabled me to see clearly the emotional quality and form emanating from those who were no longer living in the physical world. Though often mistaken as such, it is neither spirits nor a spirit world that mediums and sensitives see, but another dimension where we can build with our thoughts and where the lights and colours of thought, emotion and mind become visible to us.

Some of our first glimpses of higher dimensions come through our emotional experiences. It is that bright, volatile, quicksilver emotional reality that we can peer into and beyond, through to kingdoms still higher in frequency. At times of birth, death, success, failure, pain and joy, we often, if only briefly, meet with paranormal realities that take us beyond our everyday world.

As the priest at Mass becomes inspired and meditative, his lighter self expands and explodes with breathtaking colour. And those who come from higher realms move close to us with immeasurable intensity to share in a high point of spiritual experience.

The White Misty Lady

Many powerful experiences from the first seven years of my life when we still lived in London remain vividly etched in my mind.

I remember being with my mother in the Caledonian Road, being dragged somewhat reluctantly from shop to shop along the busy street on a dark, wet, blustery day.

Quite spontaneously, my gaze was directed to a lady standing a few yards ahead of us. She was looking into the window of a furniture shop, a tall thin figure with a rather sad air. I remember clearly her headscarf framing her thin face. A strange white haziness appeared in what I now know to be a part of her aura and energy field, spreading upwards from the bottom of the oval shape, like slowly rising bubbles in a bottle of lemonade. I could hear it sizzle as it grew, until the whole ball around her was filled with a grey-white light. Then, what I can only describe as a wriggling lightning-like flash raced up her spine, disappearing into her head.

Immediately, she became rigid and stiff and keeled over, falling to the floor as she writhed grotesquely on the damp pavement.

A crowd gathered and I was whisked quickly past by my mother. As I looked back, the activity around the lady continued, the white mistiness began to give way to first a deep red and black light, followed by a pink light as her body ceased to spasm and twitch.

When later I asked what had happened, through the usual ambiguities offered me in place of an explanation, I discovered the woman was epileptic and had been experiencing a milder form of epileptic fit.

Now as I look back with acquired knowledge and experience, I realise this was my first conscious view of the mystical Kundalini, the electrical and magnetic current that continually flows snakelike along our spinal columns. Sometimes these forces race too quickly and suddenly from bottom to top, causing disruptions in the brain and nervous system, resulting in epilepsy, cerebral haemorrhage, migraine, an asthmatic or heart attack.

The white misty turbulence around this poor lady was a signal that some excessive eruption of this energy had been triggered at the more subtle level and in a moment or two it would affect her brain and body. The trigger may well have been the bright lights in the shop window reflecting on the wet paving stones.

Recently there has been a recognition of the fact that, because animals are so sensitive to changes the subtle energies precipitate in us, specially trained dogs can have a role in helping severe epileptics and those prone to similar disruptions, for they are aware of potential fits, anything up to half an hour before they manifest.

Fairies

In the drab greyness of post-war London, I grew to love our little garden. It was a haven, a safe and special place in a busy city, and I cherished the days I was able to sit on the grass in the sunshine, to look at the flowers and explore the world of insects and the magic of the natural world.

My mother, a wonderful, caring lady, managing an unusual, often difficult, child, encouraged a belief in the unseen in certain respects, as long as it did not undermine the teachings of the church. Like many people of Irish decent, she was intrigued by the mysterious, yet devoted to the mystical, as decreed by the priest and the church, and my childhood was a strange web of contradictions.

One summer, I was encouraged to participate in a game. I would leave my little green-enamel watering can in the garden before going to bed and in the morning, I would rush out to discover that the fairies, without fail, had left me some flowers, tucked into the can. Such excitement — the thrill is still with me.

Then one day, in autumn, I was going to leave my watering can in the garden again. My mother looked at me with unease in her eyes and I knew something was wrong.

'There are no fairies,' she declared. 'It was me who put the flowers in the can. You are a big boy now and you must know the truth or people will laugh at you.'

I remember the horror and disbelief I felt as my dream was shattered. My mother's face, distorted through the tears that filled my eyes, still haunts me a little.

What she had not understood and could not have known was that I had seen the fairies. I knew they were real. Always in the garden, around the flowers and especially the great lilac tree in the corner, I would watch the busy, dancing lights as they worked and played. They had no wings as such, and no faces or legs as described in mythology, but their light was clear for me to see. I saw them, as I saw the sheaths of radiance around flowers, trees, insects, animals and people. The balls of colour were there, bright, clear and alive.

The fairies and elemental energies may not have cut the flowers for me, but they were there, sure enough. Why hadn't mother realised? I'd thought everyone knew! And so I learned a major, this time painful, lesson: I must keep such things to myself unless I am sure others will understand.

I didn't leave the watering can out again with its precious request. But the fairy lights never faded away.

A Vision of Anger

The visions of children are often dismissed by their older, wiser parents. We reject them as being without meaning or as fantasy when a child shares an insight that doesn't fit our logical understanding.

Dad, who loved his 'pint', would often introduce to me someone he had recently met saying this was 'uncle' this or 'uncle' that, usually as I ate crisps and drank Tizer outside a local pub in King's Cross, where my paternal grandmother lived.

On one occasion I was introduced to such a man, who smiled at me as I backed off from him. I was very uneasy with him and didn't share my father's enthusiasm for his new pal. Around the man I could see a mass of swirling colours, predominantly reds, dirty browns and black-aubergine, and some of the light formed into fast-moving jagged lines.

To recoil from such a vision was a natural thing to do, yet, on the surface, the man seemed pleasant enough and my father was just a little embarrassed at his son's reticence to embrace this new-found friend.

But some weeks later, this same man was caught by the police after battering a neighbour and stealing from their house. I had learned very early that the colours never lie, even when the face does!

Atmospheres and the Solar Plexus

Most of us are familiar with the reaction in our stomach and its nerve plexus when we receive exciting or sad news or are suddenly exposed to a new experience.

During my childhood, we would often travel by tube. I usually enjoyed it, but at times I would become agitated while waiting on the platform, deep below ground. The drawing sensations in my stomach were terribly compulsive and I would feel a strong pull towards the edge of the platform, though this was nothing to do with the down-draught caused by the trains. It was only in adult life that I was able to see and better understand the lines of force and energy that squeezed through the tunnels.

The whole London Underground system works like a giant magnetic field and, because the Underground network is well below the earth's surface, the natural magnetic charge given off by the rail network amplifies powerful earth energies. While these are quite beautiful forces, they affect us all in many different ways and can have an awesome and even overwhelming effect.

Excessive exposure can lead to fatigue, depression, anxiety and panic, and a vortex is sometimes created into which the less resilient among us are drawn.

The forces disrupt the chakras or energy centres around our bodies (we look at these in detail later), especially the solar plexus, located in the stomach area. To highly sensitive people and children, the experience can be very uncomfortable; it is more noticeable when we are tired and blood sugar is low, making the solar plexus more vulnerable.

Because children have a particular sensitivity in the solar plexus chakra, the foods they usually enjoy most, high in refined sugars that exhaust the pancreas, make matters worse. The result is often illogical, strange or unruly behaviour, hyperactivity and fear or panic attacks, conditions that have no obvious cause.

My behaviour was always at its worst and my feelings most difficult to manage when I had received a fix of sugars in sweets and drinks. My ability to cope with atmospheres as a child was most erratic. This is a problem that parents continue to address today as children's sensitivity to toxins, and their inability to process the physical and subtle toxins we surround them with, increases.

Night Visitors

We all have powerful night-time dreams at some time or another. They are part of our psychic experience and our frequent, if confused, contact with the fourth dimension, known as the emotional or astral plane. When we go to sleep, our higher selves leave our physical bodies and the physical plane and align with the non-physical collective emotions and thoughts that surround our earth and humanity. These are the experiences we call our nightmares.

As a child, I was a vivid dreamer, often disturbing my parents as I encountered fearful monsters and terrifying events. Often enough, I was described as highly strung or neurotic, as having an overactive imagination, but, like most children whose contact with the more subtle realms and those fourth, fifth and sixth dimensions is very powerful, I was simply open to some of the confusing thought forms or structures that radiate through the lower levels of the astral plane. It is a world of contrasts, powerful images and fast-changing experiences and feelings.

One experience, which was puzzling at the time, and which I kept to myself once my parents had dismissed it as fantasy, occurred when I was around seven years old. It was a dream-like encounter that was different to all those I have had, both before and since.

My sleep was disturbed by an extremely bright light that filled my bedroom. The place was alive with this clear, white light which was fringed in places with pink and red patches.

And I remember a strange smell around me, like burnt cabbage, coming from the edge of my bed.

I could see two small figures facing me, about four feet or so high. They were brownish grey, with peculiar little shiny bodies and disproportionately large, oval heads. Their eyes were dark and slanted; they had small stubby nostrils; their fingers were long and thin. The figures gazed at me, occasionally turning their heads to look at each other as if in silent communication.

I was terrified, and powerless. I couldn't shout or scream. I felt stuck to the bed, gripped by a strange paralysis. All attempts to move proved completely futile.

The two creatures came up to me, held my arms firmly and moved me out of my bed. Everything seemed to be in slow-motion. We crossed to the side of the room, one on either side of me, still holding my arms. I was rigid with fear. I couldn't understand why no one else in the house was aware of what was going on. Why couldn't they hear anything? Suddenly the light in the room changed to blue. I felt the two creatures start as it did so, and in front of us stood two other entities, quite different in appearance.

These were very tall, seven or eight feet at least, and I could discern no perfume or odour as I had from the others. They were a pale blue colour, apparently dressed in white garments. Immediately, my arms were released and it seemed some intense dialogue was taking place between the two sets of strange visitors. I couldn't hear any speech, yet I was somehow aware of negotiations taking place around me.

During this strange, silent dialogue, I had felt excited yet no longer really afraid. It was all like a dream, yet somehow more real. Even now, as I think of it, I can feel the grip of the two little creatures on my arms and can smell their strange scent.

Then, briefly, it seemed I was somehow transferred or lifted to a playground or park where I could play on the swings and roundabouts for a time. I was quite alone, yet safe and comfortable. It was like the seaside, but more brightly coloured, truly psychedelic, and no one else was around. Even so, I felt secure.

Moments later, I was back in my bedroom. The little brownish-grey men had gone and the tall figures, whom I remember as having a remarkably calming presence, essentially benign, placed me back in my bed.

Once again, without any audible speech, they communicated to me that I was safe and would sleep now. I had nothing to fear, they said, and would receive no more such visits. I think they smiled; they certainly gently stroked me, and then, quite suddenly, disappeared. The blue light faded and I remember no more.

Next morning I told my parents what had happened to me. They laughed and suggested I should never again eat cheese before going to bed! The memory sank deep into my subconscious until many years later. It was just a dream. Or was it?

Lightning Strikes

Adolescence was a wonderful time for me and, like most, I can recall that tentative yet exciting progression towards manhood, searching to realise who I was, and also why I was. Between the ages of eleven and seventeen, my life revolved heavily around my connections with the youth organisation, the Boys Brigade, to which I am eternally grateful for the many happy years and experiences I had within its influence. The playing in the bugle band, the classes and especially the summer camps were a great feature of the time.

I was sixteen and camping on a clifftop at Holland-on-Sea, Essex, with a large group of boys from several Boys Brigade companies. The weather had been reasonably bright with strong sunshine for the opening days, but one day in particular became grey and overcast. Not everyone was on camp at the time and a few of us more senior lads were supervising basic 'fatigues' for the day — peeling potatoes, clearing up the site and generally ensuring the preparation of the meals was undertaken properly.

When there was a pause in the chores, a few of us who were close friends would take some moments together to chat or maybe play cards. On this particular day, there was a poignant atmosphere on the campsite and a pervasive heaviness all around. Several times that morning I shook my head as a strange whistling sound like a fast, rushing wind seemed to brush past my ears, leaving me giddy and with a peculiar sense of imminence in my heart, for what I could not tell.

I can still hear the rumbling as the thunderstorm began and the wall of hailstones spread menacingly like a marching army towards us. We ran for shelter into one of the bell tents and, when settled, began a game of cards.

I leaned against the large wooden pole in the centre of the tent as I viewed my cards with disdain. What a poor hand — I had no chance of winning! I was about to play my card, when the whistling sound that had haunted me started up again. Immediately, I felt an earwig crawling on my leg and I went to brush it away. But as I tried to move my hand, there was a great blue-white flash beside me and my pals. Everything in me seemed virtually paralysed and it seemed that those few seconds lasted for ages.

'Down, Lamby. Down!' One of my pals leaned heavily on me and we curled up together in this strange experience. We didn't know what was happening and didn't even hear the thunder that must have accompanied this great bolt of lightning.

I remember now, the dream beyond the experience, a shift into the brightly coloured world of the astral light. I was a child, surrounded by ice cream, psychedelic coloured toys, images and patterns. An image: my Great Grandmother — 'Go back!' she said. And with a growing smell of scorched rubber in my head I re-entered my physical shell as it juddered and shook. For a moment, I thought I was in my bedroom at home, but the stench of burning was so great it dragged me back to reality.

I was burned and paralysed yet lucky to be alive. So too were all my friends — lucky to be conscious again and breathing. None of the others were paralysed, but the bolt of lightning had struck nearest to me and it burned my flesh, singed all my body hairs, drained the blood from my limbs and even melted my nylon socks.

But I could see so much. In the delirium as we called out for help (surprisingly, no one else on the site realised that we had been hit) the tent seemed to be filled with entities from other realms, touching us and somehow sustaining us until we were taken to hospital. They were silver, gold and blue; tall, shining figures I now understand to be angelic beings and relatives from higher planes, expressing concern for our plight.

I knew then that we would all recover.

The Nurse's Halo

As we were cared for in the hospital during our recovery from our ordeal and my near-death experience, we enjoyed a little celebrity, as survival of such a close encounter with lightning is rare. And it appeared my encounter was the most intimate, with the temporary paralysis and quite remarkable burns, one of which left a beautiful fern-leaf imprint on my stomach and rib cage.

Many curious medics paid me a visit as I lay in bed in shock, with a very high temperature, one even photographed the burn. But I just wanted to be left alone to rest. Realising my distress, a little Irish nurse came over to admonish yet another inquisitive group of junior doctors, more interested in science than healing, as they requested a view of my now famous inflamed skin.

'Let the boy have some peace, he could have died,' she said as she brushed past them, wiped my brow and settled me in my bed. The light around her head was beautiful — a true sister of mercy.

I can still picture the rich, deep blue aura around her shoulders and framing her red-cheeked face; the radiant gold and purple patches floating across it; and the beams of silver, gold, white and green pouring from the crown of her head like magic beams of some special moonlight. I didn't realise it consciously at the time, but here was a lady of prayer and devotion, truly in touch with her higher self and very much in tune with the needs of others.

With her around, I felt safe, and certain that the bigger plan was truly in operation through the golden glow in her heart.

CHAPTER 2
THE LIGHT OF AURAS

There was a time, when meadow, grove and stream,
The earth, and every common sight, to me did seem
Apparelled in celestial light ...
William Wordsworth

The world we live in exists at many levels and, for most people, the physical world is the 'real' world. However, the physical world only exists because it is supported by many other intricate layers. These layers can be understood as other dimensions or planes of being.

We radiate the most complex and wonderful patterns and forms of light. Most religious books of various orthodoxes refer to light as an attribute of mankind and say that this is our true nature.

In adolescence I frequently observed light emanating from physical entities. People often shone for me, flowers radiated, rooms filled with colour, songs released bubbles of iridescence into the air and towns glowed with bands of fascinating energy. It was a colourful life!

I found my approaching early adolescent experience full of exciting fun and possibilities and intense, powerful feelings. The first days at Grammar School, the music of the choir, so unlike any singing I had listened to before. The colours flowing through the school hall as the boys' voices rose and blended together, rather like bubbles coming from the mouths of pouting fish.

I loved to sing and I remember my excitement at being given a place in this excellent school choir. It was a real privilege and music was a very important aspect of school life.

One particular morning has a very special and powerful place in my memory and in my spiritual unfoldment. I sat in my usual spot amongst my pals during morning service. As the organ played and we all stood up to sing, several remarkable things happened.

The hymn, 'From Glory to Glory', was one I especially loved, very powerful and stirring and still a favourite to this day. We sang it with verve and enthusiasm. The release of devotional energy mixed with boyish exuberance must have heightened my awareness. As I write these words and my memory serves up the delights of that special moment, I wish I could savour the experience again.

Around each boy and teacher, I saw two oval fields of coloured light, pulsing with gently flowing tones and hues and seeming to spin in opposite directions. One oval was slightly larger than the other and the two rotated at different speeds. Inside these remarkable forms the colours shimmered and radiated, changing and moving, first one way, then the next. The obvious underlying pattern of colour in each sphere was continually being modified as the singing progressed. It was a most spectacular and inspiring sight.

My jaw dropped when, from the crowns of several heads, sparkling light strands of silver and deep violet darted upwards and outwards, like the most remarkable firework displays I had seen.

One or two boys had curious blue transparent spheres around their necks and throats and similar but different ones around their chests and hearts. The balls seemed to turn and move, the colours becoming more evident as the singing became more powerful and emotionally charged. Some subtle kind of light crescendo was building in tandem with the singing.

As the hymn ended and the prayers went on, so everything dimmed and assumed its more normal, or rather, to me, more usual vibrant, appearance.

While at that time my glimpses of the subtle fourth- and fifth-dimensional realms were becoming more controllable than in my earlier years and could usually be threaded through my mind like a subliminal film, I also had exceptionally powerful, spontaneous visions like this one, and I can see now how it was all part of a very special learning process, taking me towards something that I would grow to understand and put to good use later. Somehow, my mind was being calibrated for the future.

These experiences were always interesting, sometimes startling, yet I had learned not to share them, in spite of an almost uncontrollable urge, a surging impulse within me. Others would find me either foolish or insane and I could not risk anyone trampling on my precious, dazzling world. It was too beautiful for that.

Auric Layers

My subtle vision was revealing what I subsequently came to know as the light of the emotions and the mind in the human aura. If we take the nature of man to be essentially spiritual, our physical body is the material imprint of a great spiritual creature, living and working on earth, and around and interwoven with the physical body are several layers of light, often referred to as subtle bodies.

The two ovals I had been seeing were the colours shown by individuals as their feelings and thoughts change and unfold. The smaller, inner field, is generally called the emotional or astral body and the outer field, the mental body (see Figure 1). Both have vivid colours of differing intensities radiating through them, and I often observe how the light of the larger, mental oval is always different to that of the astral form. It is less volatile, less

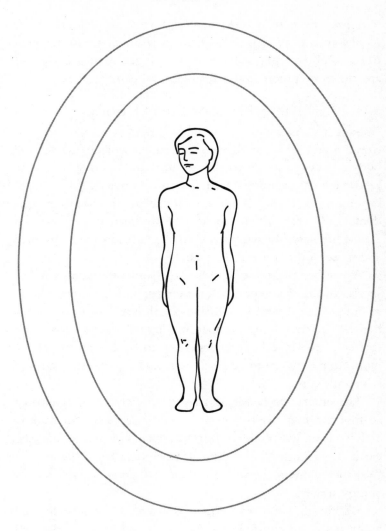

*Figure 1 The physical body surrounded by the emotional,
or astral, body and the mental body.*

like quicksilver in its movement and there are colours in the mental body for which we have no correspondence in the spectrum of normal physical vision. The larger, mental body also appears to spin more slowly than its astral partner.

The Etheric, or Energy, Body

The etheric, energy or vitality body (I tend to use the first two names more) is the matrix or pattern upon which your physical body is built and structured. It surrounds and interpenetrates the physical body, seeming to stretch some three to four inches beyond it (see Figure 2). On the surface are the strands or conductors of force, which radiate into the planetary ethers and enable the flow of energy between the individual's energy field and those of the sun and the planet.

As we breathe, these strands also channel the energy into a myriad of absorption points, some corresponding with the pores of our skin, so we can literally breathe through the tissue of our bodies. The strands are grouped in clusters of seven across the surface of the etheric body and seem to be a vital part of the interaction between the etheric body and the etheric planes in which it exists.

The etheric body has four layers, or frequencies, and they all fuse together to produce the vitality necessary for healthy activity. It draws in energy from the ethers of the sun and the earth (see Figure 3). As we breathe, we breathe in the etheric substance which enters our bodies as etheric particles, or energy spirals.

On a bright summer's day, there is an abundance of vitality and you can see this clearly if you look for it. Sit back or relax and look up into a sunny sky (but not directly at the sun). In your vision, you will see thousands of small, tadpole-like spots, darting back and forth. These are the etheric or energy particles, which pulse around you and in everyone, flowing through your etheric

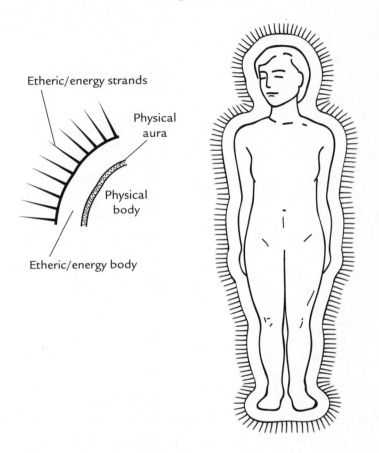

Etheric/energy strands

Physical
aura

Physical
body

Etheric/energy body

Figure 2 The physical body surrounded by the etheric, or energy, body.

body. These energising particles are at their most abundant at around 2 p.m. on a summer's day. They gradually diminish in quantity until around 2 a.m., when the available energy around us is at its lowest. It is interesting that 2 a.m. is a 'popular' time for natural death in older people, when vitality is at its lowest and the etheric body is depleted, less able to hold on to the physical frame it supports and nourishes.

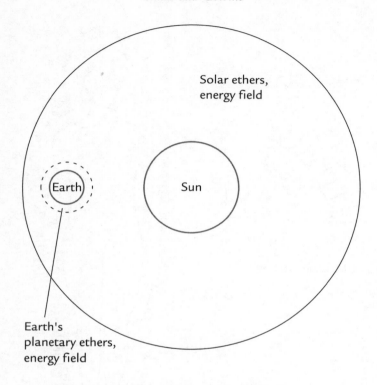

Figure 3 The energy fields of the sun and the earth.

On occasions when you feel tired and need a boost to your vitality, look at these energy particles and imagine them pouring into your body as you breathe. Welcome them and invite them in to energise you. Your energy will then rise significantly as you feel the steady, beautiful flow of vitality coming into your body, nourishing it and strengthening it. I have used this exercise effectively with many individuals who were suffering from fatigue and conditions like M.E., as they seek to increase and sustain higher, more normal, levels of energy.

The energy particles appear to enter the etheric body as we breathe, predominantly through a series of spinning vortices

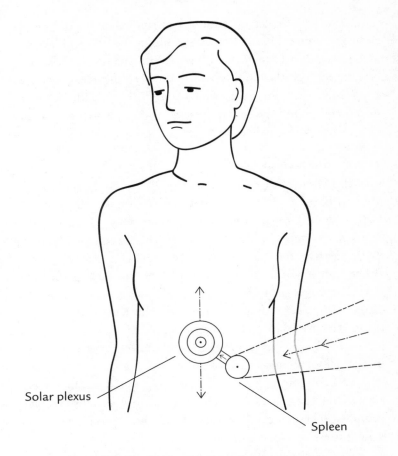

Solar plexus

Spleen

*Figure 4 Absorption of etheric energy, via the spleen and
solar plexus chakras, into the spinal system.*

along its surface (the psychic centres or chakras), the principle
one being located at the back of the body, opposite the spleen.
The energy is channelled to the solar plexus and continues, from
there, to spread vitality, via the spinal system, into every area of
the etheric body, and finally into the glands of the physical body
(see Figure 4).

On one particular occasion I was singing in a professional choir in a concert in the Purcell Rooms of the Queen Elizabeth Hall in London. One of the soloists, a fine singer from Australia, was singing very beautifully and I could see the acceleration of the vitality that was being drawn into her body through the spleen chakra and two other vortices as she approached the climax of her performance.

Etheric doubles, or counterparts

In each etheric body there is a matrix which corresponds to the physical body in all its detail, with an etheric double or counterpart for each organ, limb, and so on. So, where there is a liver, there is an energy form like a liver; where there are kidneys, there are two transparent glass-like kidneys in energy form. When the physical form is damaged or gone altogether, the etheric counterpart remains completely intact and in place. This explains why, for example, in patients who have had a limb or organ removed, they can often still feel the limb to be present. This also has a powerful implication, for it means that the capacity to regrow organs and limbs exists. Our belief systems and conditioning have dismissed this as a possibility and it is rarely acknowledged. My belief is that organ and tissue regeneration will be one day be accepted and understood. The potential exists — it is merely dormant.

I also believe that the success of organ transplants is inhibited because donated organs have an alien quality and resonance that does not match its counterpart in the etheric body of the individual. Thus, the etheric forces precipitate the rejection of organs and we counter or suppress this through drugs. When discussing this on one of my advanced-study courses, a doctor attending the course mentioned an interesting case where a transplant patient had severe rejection problems that were improved considerably when she meditated upon the donor's soul and thanked it for the gift of the organ. It would seem that this might be one solution to cases of acute rejection of transplanted organs.

These etheric energy forms exist around and through all physical forms — animals, flowers, plants, rocks, furniture, buildings — everything. Wherever there is matter, an etheric structure is woven into it.

Our physical health is dependent on the maintenance of a good flow of vitality through our etheric bodies and the two most important things we can do in this respect are to learn to breathe properly and to exercise often (Exercise 4 is a good foundation on which to base further study). Other issues, of course, are involved in the maintenance of good health — good management of emotions (the emotional or astral body), clear and constructive thinking (the mental body) and an openness to our souls or higher selves established through prayer and meditation.

Miasms

In the etheric body, there are frequencies or vibrations that are particular to each individual. As well as having in them the perfect pattern for the physical body to form, they also have weaknesses.

These weaknesses are referred to as miasms. Miasms are genetic tendencies or dispositions to certain types of disease that we inherit from our forebears. There is a complex theoretic structure in relation to miasms that is taught in homoeopathy, radionics and other forms of energy-based healing methods. It is sufficient here to indicate that these miasms exist and are perceptible in the etheric body. But what is more important is that a balanced, healthy lifestyle with good attitude and thinking can and does neutralise these patterns and enables us to live longer and healthier lives — we do not need to be slaves to our past or our ancestry. Most of us can recognise tendencies to certain conditions in ourselves and in our families, but we have a responsibility to break the thinking patterns and behaviours that reinforce them and to set ourselves free.

Exercises

An etheric body is actually quite easy to see. Here are some simple exercises that you can try to begin to stimulate your etheric or energy vision. Though they are presented here in the order I would introduce them in my workshops, if you are working on your own, you may find it more convenient to try them in the order 2–3–1 so that you can gain a little confidence before you ask a friend to take part.

Exercise 1

Do this exercise with a friend in a gently lit room.

1. With your friend's back towards you, place your chair a few feet away and, with a few deep breaths, quietly take time to relax.
2. Close your eyes and think of your friend as a being of many levels, their physical form being the lowest or most dense level.
3. Keeping your eyes closed, imagine your friend's physical outline and then allow your inner eye and vision to show you their energy body. Don't be disappointed if nothing happens in early attempts — persistence and confidence are the key. You are reprogramming your subconscious, asking it to reveal what may have been hidden from you for many lifetimes! Give yourself time. The subconscious was once described to me as an old man sitting in front of the fire, slippers on, reading the paper. He's happy where he is but will take notice and move if you are persistent and consistent.
4. Slowly open your eyes and continue to relax, allowing yourself to adjust to seeing objectively again (inner vision being

subjective). Concentrate your gaze around the shoulders at first and you may detect a hazy, almost transparent, quality shimmering around the shoulders, head and neck. As the perception develops, you may see a smoky bluish colour around the physical body, about two to four inches deep or maybe even more. It may seem to vibrate or even shimmer as your friend breathes.

5. In time, you will begin to notice even the spiky radiations that stick out like hairs on a cropped head, all around the etheric or energy body.

This exercise can be repeated using animals, flowers or trees.

Exercise 2

1. Place your hands together, palm to palm, with fingertips touching.
2. Relax and take a few deep, slow breaths. Then very slowly, draw your hands apart, watching and concentrating.
3. Try to sense the bond, a kind of stickiness, between the hands and especially the fingertips. You may even see the strands of energy between your fingers and palms as you move your hands slowly apart.

Exercise 3

1. Shake your hands rapidly for a few seconds, then hold them still, palms inwards for a moment, about twelve inches apart.
2. Gradually, move your hands towards each other, feeling and sensing the change in the density of the space between them. If you practise, when the hands are about four to six inches apart, you will feel (and maybe see) a pressure or resistance between them — one of my students said it was rather like holding a balloon. Your fingers may tingle or feel hot.

As you conclude each of these exercises, and all the other exercises in the book, use the following technique to clear and radiate your energy. These steps will help you manage your awareness sensibly as it grows.

With practice, you will find the clearing and radiating exercise becomes increasingly valuable and, as you will see as you progress through the book, I start to recommend that you perform this exercise at the beginning of your attunement exercises as well as at the end. You will quickly understand its benefits and, in time, you will find you fit this activity around your other exercises very easily.

Clearing and radiating energy

Exercise 4

1. Sit quietly and relax for a moment or two. Choose a comfortable, upright chair and loosen any tight clothing.
2. Become conscious of your breathing by focusing your attention on your solar plexus and abdomen, and notice how, as you breathe, your stomach and abdomen rise upwards and then fall gently back down as you exhale.
3. Slow your breathing down a little by saying very slowly in your head, 'I breathe in,' pause, 'I breathe out,' and pause again. Continue to keep your attention on your stomach and abdominal movements as you do this and gradually you will establish a slow, gentle rhythm in your breathing, bringing more energy into your body. Never force your breathing in any way; always allow your progress to be gradual and gentle. You will also, with regular practice, be able to count the breaths in and out for up to six seconds each, with a gentle pause after each movement, first while the breath is in the body and then when it has been expelled. This is rhythmic breathing.
4. Next, imagine a beautiful clear energy filling your body as you breathe, each breath entering your body in a flowing motion through the crown of your head, and gradually filling

every part of you, relaxing your muscles, your organs and your nervous system. You are filled with energy.

5. Imagine this energy radiating through you in all directions, like a beautiful light — in front of you and behind you, to the right of you and to the left of you, above you and below you. Establish that vision in your mind.

6. Finally, take a few minutes to readjust and ground yourself properly before carrying on with everyday activites.

Always use the grounding approach that follows to help you readjust to normal consciousness whenever you are concluding exercises and activities involving sensitivity and subtle awareness. Shifts in awareness happen to us all the time, often in not-so-obvious ways, perhaps when listening to music, drawing or painting a picture, or in activities with a less physical focus or in sleep states. Being conscious of the need to ground ourselves or readjust should become a normal part of any mental or psychic routine.

Grounding

At the end of any attunement exercise, gently bring your awareness back to normal and connect with the physical everyday world by feeling your feet firmly on the ground, your chair supporting you, sensing the space and presence of the environment you are in. Do this slowly. Imagine putting your body back on as if it were a garment you had taken off for a while. (As your physical body has been 'loosened' in the activity, try to think of it as needing to fit you like a glove again once you have put it back on.)

Open your eyes slowly and awaken fully.

Saying thanks

On completion of any exercise or activity, make it also your practice to say thank you to your subconscious mind for its work in providing you with the information and insights you require. What has been revealed to you may seem small or insignificant at the time, but all good things begin small, are built up brick by brick and require patience and a calm sustained expectancy and gratitude on your part. This is a natural and powerful aspect of any psycho-spiritual work. You may thank God, the Universe, or any entity you regard as the creative aspect of life. We should never take creation for granted.

Attunement exercises and 'closing down'

All the exercises I teach in this book are safe and based on years of experience. People often ask me about 'closing down' after dealing with subtle and esoteric ideas. The truth of the matter is that it is neither possible nor desirable to close down anything or anyone in this respect. What we have to learn is basic mental and emotional, that is, psychic, hygiene, as demonstrated in Exercise 4, and also, through practice, reprogramming our subconscious response so that we adjust perfectly for whatever level of activity we are engaged in. When we finish praying we don't 'close down'; rather, we readjust to normal activity.

Practices you might come across, such as closing down, painting crosses over chakras and building shells or layers of light as a form of protection around ourselves, are all fear-driven and based on ignorance, usually taught by well-meaning individuals who do not see subtle forms clearly. If they did, they would see the consequences of their teaching, the thought forms they subsequently attract and the problems they create rather than solve.

A soundly based meditational life is an essential platform for all esoteric and spiritual study. Make it your priority and see the exercises in this book as the beginnings of a voyage of wonderful discovery and growth for you that you will never, ever regret.

The Emotional, or Astral, Body

I once worked with a teacher who seemed to be in good health and pretty much in control of his life, but I always found sitting close to him made me feel sad and even anxious, even though he may have been smiling and generally appearing quite relaxed. It came as quite a shock to his colleagues to learn that he was to be away from school for a while as he was suffering from depression and anxiety and for some considerable time had been taking prescribed medication to mask the difficulties from everyone.

When we are in close physical proximity to someone, we are also interacting with their emotional and mental selves. Sitting near to my colleague exposed me to his feelings in a very powerful way, even though my subtle vision had not given me other spontaneous signals.

This is why, if we are sensitive, we may often suffer in difficult atmospheres and environments and find some individuals draining and depressing, while other places and people inspire and uplift us. As a child, I would feel so intensely the difficult atmosphere at home after a serious argument between my parents and the subsequent hostile silences, and would welcome the often unexpected visit of an aunt or uncle, whose cheery appearance would immediately 'melt the ice' and bring better feelings to me and everyone.

The emotional or astral body is the auric layer in which our emotions operate. To me, this body appears in an oval form, with powerful, vibrant, coloured rays pulsing through it in synchronisation with the rhythm in the brain. The most dense area of this body is around the human physical body, generally becoming lighter and thinner in texture as it moves towards the edge of the oval.

The oval shape (illustrated in Figure 1) that this and the other higher bodies have, which together form the aura, is in fact illusory. The astral body does not have a shape in the commonly accepted sense and has no actual edges. It enables us to live and function in the emotional plane — the fourth dimension. But as, intellectually, we are unable easily to grasp the concept of four dimensions, the subconscious mind gives us a three-dimensional model or construct to work with — the idea that our emotions operate most dynamically within a specific form, body or space — and we can identify with this and relate to it. Occasionally, however, we may hear of an aura having tears or holes in it, but this is a rather simplistic idea and is actually incorrect, as the aura has no 'surface' in which tears and holes can form.

The apparent dimensions of the human emotional body vary, depending on the emotional state of the individuals to whom they belong. Generally, if an individual extends his or her arms sideways, straight out from the shoulder, the fingertips determine the edge of the most dynamic area of the emotional self. It appears to radiate a similar distance in front and behind the physical body, and about 12 to 16 inches above the head and below the soles of the feet.

The astral body pulses and, at the same time, seems to spin, very gently, predominantly in an anti-clockwise direction. The pulsation can be witnessed in the vivid, electric colours which are breathtaking in their translucence and vibrancy. And the magic of these great lights seems to defy description. The astral body is often described as the 'watery' plane, as the light seems to flow through it like great tides of star-like coloured force.

Colours speak

With one client, I remember trying to understand a problem she had. Her severe arthritis was like a shackle on her, placing severe limitations on her and causing her great pain. The healing and counselling I had given her was bringing some relief, but not enough. After a few days, the pain would return and the limbs would seize up again.

We discussed frankly her thoughts and feelings and I asked about her husband and the support he gave her. Did she resent him at all, for being fully mobile, active and able to live life with a freedom and energy she could only dream of? I sensed some tension as the question registered. Quite suddenly, the red and brown in the lower part of her aura began to stir. It became cloudier and the colours mixed, seeming to darken, becoming more opaque as they did so. I could detect a peculiar odour and then a powerful humming sound resonating in my head that seemed to come from these heavy, dense rays of light.

'There are times when I hate him,' she said. 'I love him but I am angry at his mobility, his coping with everything, yet, I shouldn't be. I know I shouldn't be.'

I noticed how her solar plexus chakra was spinning like a catherine wheel, yet the energy in her heart was lethargic and slow. She hunched over, as if she had a pain in her chest, but it was simply her anguish and her subconscious attempt to shield her troubled heart that I was observing.

She then burst into tears and cried for many, many minutes, like a baby, the child in her rising to the surface. Through the tears, she smiled. Her face lit up. The idealistic pale blue light began to dominate as she spoke of her dreams, her hopes. The bell-like sounds in her aura were stunning and enervating. Immediately, she could move a little better and was more relaxed.

Here the colours had literally spoken to me. I was beginning to understand their message and the information they contained that was to lead, in time, to the work I now do, helping thousands of people regain their power and grow into a more beautiful realisation of themselves.

The colours of the higher bodies are all those we can see in the physical spectrum from infra-red to ultra-violet and beyond.

I frequently observe colours for which I can see no correspondence in the spectrum of our normal vision. Sometimes the colours are smooth and at other times, patchy or blotchy, denoting certain problems or tendencies in an individual's emotional nature.

Auric awareness

Exercise 5

1. Stand or sit comfortably in the middle of a quiet room or space, where you will not be disturbed.
2. If you wish, close your eyes. Relax and slow your breathing a little, using the words, 'I breathe in,' and 'I breathe out,' as in Exercise 4.
3. Next, think of the etheric or energy matter that supports your physical body and how it is interwoven with all the other cells in your physical body. Imagine its radiation around you. Be still, sense and feel its activity; if you look, listen and wait patiently often enough your awareness will grow.
4. Feel three more slow breaths flowing through your etheric body, coming in through the spleen chakra, into the solar plexus and from there, into the whole etheric system as your body pulses and radiates.
5. Think of all the lines of force as they criss-cross around you. Remember the hair-like radiations on the surface of the etheric body as they radiate back into the energy field of the planet and solar system.
6. Next, centre your thinking inside your head, just behind and above your eyes. Allow a picture to form of a beautiful flower. Let the flower grow as its colours become more vivid, so much so that you can almost feel it and smell its fragrance. Enjoy it.
7. Think how beautiful the flower is and what a wonderful garden it is in, vibrant and alive, yet calm. As these thoughts

and feelings flow through you, enjoy them further, allowing them to flow.

8. Then remember the dimension in you that enables these feelings and emotions to flow — the emotional or astral plane. Visualise its form as it also interpenetrates your physical body and then appears to radiate from where you are standing or sitting like a great sphere of light and colour all around you. Take a deep breath, relax and enjoy the idea for a few moments.

9. Count three more slow, deep breaths, returning gradually to your physical body, putting it back on just like a garment, feeling your feet firmly upon the floor, grounded and in touch with the physical life again. Then slowly, open your eyes and be still until you feel fully connected and awake.

The Mental Body

The mental body, in its concrete, or lower, form is presented as an ovoid structure, similar to, but larger than, its emotional counterpart, as we saw in Figure 1. It too has a spinning motion and is full of colours, but with a different emphasis or mix to the astral body. In the mental body, it is clear that the colours move and pulse more slowly, rather like white fluffy clouds that float across the sky on a calm summer's day. Their motion becomes slightly more staccato and quickened at times of crisis, challenge or intense interest, where the mind is called into a higher level of activity.

The colour range and tone values are also different from three-dimensional colours and those of the astral plane, the yellows appearing much more golden or copper in hue, the blues more metallic and turquoise and the reds more crimson and cerise. Greens almost disappear from the mental body completely and there is usually little evidence of the blacks, greys and muddy browns so often seen in the emotional body, especially in the lower half of its form. There are some remarkable visual effects, best described as metallic or translucent but otherwise indefinable in normal terms; these are especially noticeable in the linear radiations around the top of the aura, which are indicative of prayer, aspiration and higher thinking. These radiations are especially linked to the crown and heart chakras.

Thought forms

Our thoughts become concrete and intellectually identifiable in the lower portion of the mental body. But they are first seen as spirals and movements of light in the rays of the mental body's oval form and then they start to form as symbols or shapes that percolate down into the emotional body. Here they resonate very vividly and as we concentrate on them they attract power, become images we can recognise and understand and are then projected with energy out into the relevant plane of consciousness, travelling along tube-like thought streams or cords to whoever or whatever identifies with them, or staying close to us until they materialise in our three-dimensional world (see Figure 5).

Most of the thought forms in the thought energy streams I have seen have fallen into one of several types (see Figure 6). The most common form I see in the mental and emotional bodies is the spiral. Spirals fly and spin like fireworks released into the night sky and they appear to have an essentially black and silver spiral core with a varying amount of star-like dust falling off them as they travel; the amount of this dust varies according to the intensity of the thought and the degree of emotional force and projection behind it. Some spirals move quite slowly, others race away into the mental planes. The dust-like matter, as if magnetic, is drawn into sympathetic auric fields where other individuals who are thinking along similar lines

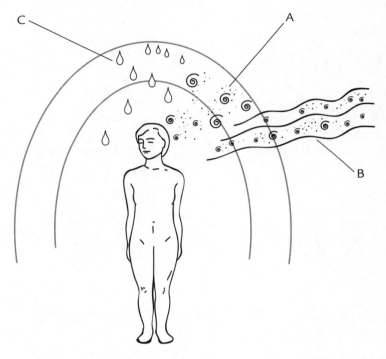

A = Thoughts spiralling as they attract energy and are released
into the mental and emotional planes

B = Thoughts spiralling into thought streams of coloured rays, as
they are then directed towards a specific goal or individual

C = Thought forms becoming accessible ideas and 'tear-dropping'
deeper into the conscious mind of the individual

Figure 5 The thought process.

will be stimulated or fuelled by them.

Another common form is the teardrop shape, which grows in
the aura as ideas become concrete and recognisable in the mind
as pictures.

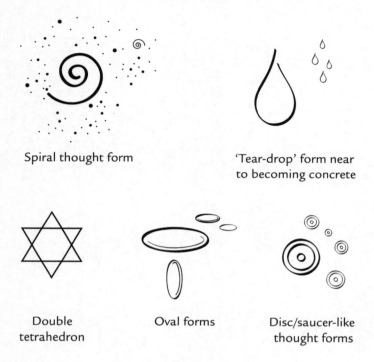

Spiral thought form

'Tear-drop' form near
to becoming concrete

Double
tetrahedron

Oval forms

Disc/saucer-like
thought forms

Figure 6 Thought forms.

At the inspirational level, there is a star-like form, usually accompanying prayer, inspiration and high spiritual ideas, always radiating upwards and downwards at the top of the aura and near the crown and heart chakras. The configuration is actually a three-dimensional star with twelve points like a double tetrahedron, but its profile is that of the six-pointed star. The stars pulse as they move in cloud formations through the mental body and also like rays in lines or streams, and generally have an extremely pale shell-like colour, occasionally looking more like pearl.

The first time I recognised the star shapes was when I saw them in my own aura. I was about ten years old and, while on holiday with my parents, I entered a talent competition. I truly enjoyed the experience, especially the audience's laughter at my jokes and funny songs and I was thrilled when I was asked to take part in the grand final. I could see clearly the star-like forms running up and down in my aura, occasionally zooming suddenly as if blasted upwards in an invisible chute. I understand now what is meant by having 'stars in your eyes'!

The other common forms are the oval and the disc, almost like a saucer of transparent china. These also seem to link with higher, creative thinking and inspired, visionary mental activity.

Thought form perception

Exercise 6

1. First practise the clearing and radiation exercise.
2. Initially, working alone, relax in your chair and reflect on the auric layers, the bodies around you — the physical, etheric, astral and mental.
3. Remember that these are your bodies, but they are NOT who you are. You respect them and utilise them for this lifetime — your physical body enables you to live in the physical world, your energy body helps you to draw on the world of power, your astral body leads you through the place of emotions and feelings and in your mental body, you dwell in the realm of thoughts and ideas.
4. Next, concentrate for a moment or two upon a particularly beautiful and tranquil image, perhaps a country scene you know well and love or the shores of a beautiful beach on a warm summer's day. See or sense the image as powerfully as you can.
5. After a few moments, allow your perception or vision to let go of your chosen image and then imagine yourself climbing up a strong, secure ladder. When at the top you are able to see clearly into your aura above your head and around

your shoulders. Observe the forms and colours you see and then slowly climb down back into your body.

6. Carefully connect again with rhythmic breathing and run through the steps of Exercise 4 before opening your eyes and returning to normal awareness.

Repeat the exercise over time, using busier or different images, each time exploring your aura with your imagination, 'climbing out' into the space for a moment or two to perceive what is going on and to witness the phenomenon of the thought forms.

You can also do this exercise to observe the thought forms of a friend — your partner imagines images for you while you focus your imagination on their auric field. They can visualise some beautiful contrasting images for you to attune to and watch. You may see pictures or images to begin with. If so, ask your mind to show you the thought form, and if you persist, it will do so.

Some people may see patterns or versions of the thought forms that vary from those I have indicated. While we should learn to control our focus to see and perceive what we seek to perceive, it is very likely that in any period of unfolding awareness other phenomena will emerge.

Always acknowledge and make a note of everything you see. The thought form structures may rapidly impress on your concrete imagination an interpretation of what they contain, so they may convert into other, less abstract symbols and pictures. Keeping a note will help you develop your own visual 'dictionary' or reference chart which will ultimately give you a language you can understand when observing thought streams and structures. Remember that the thought forms are shells or structures, mini-energy fields, containing ideas and thoughts.

Visions of the Emotional and Mental Planes

Prayer and aspiration

When I was young, I would often gasp audibly when I saw someone in prayer. My daughter Ruth, as a baby, repeated the experience when my wife and I took her into the beautiful pilgrim's chapel at Walsingham in Norfolk, England, drawing in a sharp breath when we entered the candle-lit room, where one or two people were in silent prayer and the contemplation of beautiful ideas.

Individuals in such states of aspiration become iridescent, shimmering windows of intense light, with great streams of light radiating upwards from the top of the aura, around the head and shoulders (see Plate 1). The top half or so of the aura resembles a bottle full of fizzy drink that has been shaken up and is about to burst. The aura even sounds similar to this. This is perhaps why an inspired or creatively excited person feels as if they are 'fit to burst', they feel as though they buzz with enthusiasm.

Anger

A similar explosive effect is seen in fury and anger but there are some clear differences in the aura. Instead of the vibrant blue and turquoise and pulsing rose vibrations and emanations of silver, violet and golden light, we observe deep black and grey reds with muddy olive hues and dirty browns. The strands, threads and balls of light near the head and shoulders are also not evident in the case of negative emotion, but fast-moving black- and brown-red jagged spirals become visible, like dark flashes of electricity soaring vertically up through the aura, seemingly with their source near to the base of the auric form or oval (see Plate 2).

In the angry and aggressive mode, the zigzag spirals are uneven, jagged and often broken, as if short-circuiting the energy movement across the aura. The thought spirals seem to break up around the edge as they spin, illustrating the incoherent, clouded thinking that is always a feature of anger and its accompanying fear and frustration.

I once visited the house of a friend whose daughter was sitting quietly in the corner as we entered the sitting room. Immediately, I could see the jagged forms in her aura, indicating fear and anger; it was like the image from a cartoon comic where the illustrators clearly draw on their subconscious imagination to suggest emotions in their characters (how close they are sometimes in their symbolism!). My friend later told me a sad account of how his daughter had been beaten physically by other young teenage girls at school earlier that day and had run away for a time. The aura showed it clearly, although it was some hours after the events had transpired. This shows how shock and negative thought patterns can linger long after the event that triggered them.

If the individual is excited and anxious, the deep fiery red also forms into blocks, brick-like structures which 'freeze' in the aura around the head (see Plate 3).

Depressive states, alcoholism and drug addiction

Pat was a very smart, intelligent woman in her late thirties. She had come to see me because her business, which she ran with her husband, was in dire straits and they were on the verge of bankruptcy. She wanted some advice on whether there was any sign in her auric pattern that could be of help to her.

However, she was heavily depressed by her long-standing, difficult circumstances and this produced some very interesting phenomena in her aura; the energy patterns around her made it very difficult for even an experienced individual to look into it clearly. As is often the case in such circumstances, Pat wanted help but did not want to hear advice that may be painful.

I am sure most people can relate to this through situations that they, or others they have known, have experienced, where depression has made them feel imprisoned and trapped. A normally invisible barrier is felt that, in chronic cases, becomes very difficult to breach.

In such depressive states, the aura flushes up with deep black-reds, often well above the centre, and a bar-like formation appears, gradually tightening and shrinking the aura and making the patient inaccessible (see Plate 4). The more chronic the depression, the more vivid the bars appear, sometimes seeming to radiate throughout the aura. As the situation improves, the bars break up forming loose masses of black, confetti-like energy, seeking to fall to the bottom of the aura to release the individual from their mental and emotional prison.

I have also noticed, when observing such phenomena, how much depressive states are implosions of anger energy that is out of control and, finding no creative focus, is turned in on the individual.

Similar patterns emerge with alcohol and drug addiction. The auric field becomes filled with the colours usually found in swamps, black olive hues, and dark, muddy browns, overlaid with twisting strands of black and grey-black distorted energy. The 'black clouds' and 'violent flashes' that are common traits in such people are clearly visible in their auric fields.

The aura of an alcoholic
The aura of an alcoholic is interesting, but unwelcoming. As well as the emotional body producing an overlay of dark, menacing spirals and flashes, similar to that of a depressive, there are aspects of the etheric or energy body that are very noticeable.

As alcohol takes hold, it affects the capacity of the solar plexus and spleen chakras to synthesise energy adequately, resulting in liver toxicity, pancreas exhaustion and possible diabetes. This has the effect of literally shrinking the etheric layers or appearing to tighten them. In turn, this places pressure in the abdominal chakra, resulting in excessive kidney (diuretic) activity. The physical body itself then feels increasingly 'tight' and heavy. (This may be where the expression 'tight' comes from, when describing someone who has had too much alcohol to drink.)

The best remedies are good sound breathing, the gradual input of natural sugars in the form of fruit and vegetables and drinking plenty of water. The use of Dr Bach's Rescue Remedy also slows down the solar plexus, helping the quick assimilation of energy to balance and clear toxins in the liver.

For those who are dependent on alcohol or drugs of any kind, both prescribed or otherwise, the regular practice of of the clearing and radiating exercise to accompany any other expert counselling and professional therapeutic support will be of great value in reducing unwanted addictions.

Bringing Light and Healing

We can seek to assist an individual in difficult circumstances in gently raising their consciousness, to bring a little light and healing into their lives. It will remind them of something special and beautiful beneath the surface of their troubled personality and life.

Exercise 7

1. Sit quietly on your own for a few minutes. Relax and prepare yourself using Exercise 4.
2. When you sense and know the light is radiating from you, imagine that in the space around your heart, there is a beautiful ball of light, full of the most wonderful colours imaginable — greens, roses, silvers, blues, all colours. This

light is a vision of the abundant light of love in your heart for others, so acknowledge it as such.

3. Next, allow this light to expand and radiate in wonderful rays, towards your friend in need, who you can now picture in your mind.

4. As you see and imagine the rays from your heart meet and touch your friend, the hidden, clear light in their own aura will begin to emerge, clearing the limiting forms and forces in their aura, and in their minds as well.

    (Always remember that the aura is a visible aspect of a deeper counterpart, in this case, the mind and feelings of another.)

5. Imagine the light glowing beautifully through your friend for a few moments (it does not have to be too long), then release the image with a 'thank you', knowing that the beautiful wisdom in the other individual will have been stimulated by your heartfelt recognition of it.

    This is a real act, not just a fantasy. It is a very powerful and beautiful gift you can offer another.

6. Next, go through the clearing and radiation exercise again before slowly returning to normal consciousness but, just before opening your eyes, focus on the Angel of Being within your friend. This is a beautiful creature which will seek to manage and integrate the light of the various bodies in the individual. Also, in your own words, ask it for help in revealing the true beauty and wisdom in your friend, that they may be healed and realise that they are loved.

Perhaps not immediately, but eventually, this approach will always have an effect of a beneficial kind. In such exercises you are not seeking control of another, you are uplifting them and offering your support as they cope with whatever stresses they face.

Imagination

You will notice how I sometimes encourage you to 'see' the idea
or whatever is the focus of an exercise. Many in the past have
dismissed what I see and understand as 'a figment of the imagination'. Well, the truth of the matter is that they are right. As you
will discover as you work through this book, your imagination
is your 'imaging facility', it is the creative tool of your spirit and
your soul — you use it all the time, even to create your outer
world, your physical reality. Feel good about imagining, it is part
of your life and therefore the universe. God 'imagined' you and
me and 'made us in his own image'. We are all part of a divine
imagination.

Auras and Remedies

Currently, the growth of non-orthodox health care is touching
the lives of almost everyone. Alternative and complementary
therapies abound. Many of them, such as herbalism, massage,
dietary therapy, osteopathy and so on, fit fairly comfortably into
the model of understanding that we already have, as it stands to
reason that plants, touch and manipulation can all be understood
to affect our physical bodies.

However, many forms of treatment such as homoeopathy,
the Bach Flower Remedies and mental and spiritual healing
have no conventionally acceptable chemical or physical, and
therefore no scientific, basis for their effectiveness. Many rationalist scientists dismiss such concepts out of hand.

Any analysis of a homoeopathic remedy, for example, will
quickly reveal only sugar, or maybe a little alcohol and water,
but certainly no chemical trace of the original drug or substance after which the remedy is named. This is because the
homoeopathic process with its many dilutions and shakings
(called succussions) leaves the energy of the substance in the
pill or tincture, but not the chemicals — they have disappeared.

It is a fascinating sight to see the waves of energy that ripple through the auric field as the energy of such a remedy takes effect. These ripples run through the colour and light of aura and remain visible for days, weeks and even months after the remedy has been accepted by the recipient. I have seen some remedies active up to two years later in the patient, the energy body especially still vibrating with the effect.

And I use the word 'accepted' deliberately, for I observed a therapist in Germany on one occasion dispensing some homoeopathic drops onto the tongue of a patient. The light in the patient's aura began to vibrate even before the droplet hit the tongue while it was still in the tiny space between the tongue and the dropper. In some way or another, we accept the droplet or pill and then the remedy becomes active in us — it does not necessarily become active at the moment it is inside our own energy field as one might expect. There is a point at which the subconscious of the patient allows the homoeopathic energy to become active — an acceptance.

Auras within auras: a note on confidentiality

It is not unusual for me to be consulted by medical professionals, and many doctors, in both the UK and overseas, have become clients and friends. I was speaking to two medical practitioners, a husband and wife, who had come to see me. During the course of the appointment, I was asked to consider issues in the lives of their children. As the questions were asked, so the picture of the relevant aura appeared before me until they hung in space, in line together, glowing, pulsing and turning. Subsequently, I was able to give them advice and counsel and it was the first occasion where I had 'tested' this particular aspect of the vision I had. Through one aura, it is possible to observe the energy pattern of any other individual they know and mention to me. It is not even necessary for me to have that person's name.

It is a particularly effective and frequently helpful process but it must only ever be used within the bounds of confidentiality. All of my work is confidential. Often I am the only person to share the information revealed by a client; even their family and friends may be unaware of the problem or issue that has come to light. And my own family and friends do not become party to what my clients discuss with me. I also treat my work with absolute discretion and will not use my abilities to spy or intrude upon another's life. I always emphasise on my courses that confidentiality is paramount and that gaining permission from all individuals concerned before viewing and reading the light of another is essential. In this way, I do not allow my perception to be used unethically.

I am regularly consulted by businessmen and people in very powerful and influential positions at national and international levels, and the emphasis of my work is always on how I can help the individual to work creatively and intuitively through their own lives and circumstances. Where I give advice to the director of a large commercial company, for example, I will only allow discussion of the patterns of any of his or her staff as a psychologist would a psychometric test, relating specifically to suitability for a position or promotion. Personal matters are not viewed or discussed at such times unless permission has been sought and obtained from the individual concerned.

Soul Lights and Babies

Another fascinating phenomenon of being able to see auric fields is that we can see the souls of children that may be born to an individual. There are often several vibrant balls of light visible in the aura of a young woman (and mature women, to a lesser extent) indicating the attachment of souls to the person and a preparedness and possible desire to incarnate through that individual. Not all the souls visible will make the journey into this physical life and some may have one or two attempts before they are successful.

One young woman in great distress came from Liechtenstein to see me. She had recently miscarried when fairly well advanced in her pregnancy and feared she may never carry a child safely at all. I first reassured her that I could see the light of that soul, vibrant and powerful near to her in her aura. I was also sure that it would come again and incarnate successfully, as would, I felt, the other two lights of souls I could see with her.

A year or so later, the soul did come and join her and her husband; since then, one of the others I saw has come too and it is quite possible that one day the third soul may also get its opportunity.

A Most Beautiful Light

While my awareness allows me to choose which level of life I attune to, I am frequently prompted to view an interesting formation of colours in the aura and energy movements of a particular individual I meet socially or professionally. Usually it is because my subconscious feels that I need to see and understand something new, to gain a fresh insight or have a firmer grasp of the reasons behind an individual's actions or behaviour.

Standing in the queue at a supermarket checkout is rarely anyone's idea of fun, but on one particular occasion, it provided me with a remarkable opportunity to broaden my knowledge and gain a deeper insight.

While I was chatting and comparing supermarket shopping to the good old days of corner shops, my eye was drawn to an extremely powerful light somewhere in the queue in front of me. I couldn't quite see who it was emanating from, but I was sure that the beautiful shimmering gold, silver and turquoise radiance indicated I was standing not too far from a very special and interesting soul, some evolved entity. It crossed my mind that maybe Mother Teresa or some other saint-like creature had nipped into Sainsbury's to do their shopping!

I shuffled around, stretching my neck to see who it was that radiated such an amazing light. To my surprise, I could see a young person with Down's syndrome. I was astounded, for the implications of this were really quite considerable.

I had always rather dismissed the idea that evolved souls would choose to incarnate upon the earth in a limited mental form, such as in one with Down's syndrome. Yet my perceptions were teaching me otherwise. Here was the aura and light of a truly remarkable entity. I wondered how many more there might be like this, walking the earth, living what appeared, at least in human terms, a relatively restricted existence, yet clearly able to learn and give so much.

Does this mean that those individuals who appear to be most sophisticated and developed when using conventional human criteria such as intelligence, creativity, eloquence, wit, are in fact not necessarily the true spiritual giants of our age?

The experience certainly prompted me to reconsider my view and to find out more about how we can all make a valuable contribution to life, however we choose to be incarnated.

CHAPTER 3

COLOURS, RAYS AND MEANINGS

The most beautiful thing we
can experience is the mysterious ...
to know that what is impenetrable really exists,
manifesting itself as the highest wisdom
and the most radiant beauty which
our dull senses can comprehend ...
Albert Einstein

A Quickening Unfoldment

During my thirties and early forties, my abilities to help others grew steadily. I learned that the coloured lights and rays I had always seen had definable meaning and could be understood and explained.

I discovered that these meanings could be established and clarified by engaging in a dialogue or conversation with them — they would speak to me, giving me information and, if I did a brief illustration of what I saw as I spoke, the rays were stimulated positively by my thought and in turn the client received a creative input quite separate from any information I was able to give to them verbally. In effect, a healing can take place.

I remember the auric light of one Hari Krishna devotee who had come for an appointment. Sitting opposite to me in his long robes, he wriggled and shifted with a little agitation as I drew the form I could see and put down the colours. After a time he began to giggle and smile: 'As you look at me and draw my colours,' he said, 'I feel as if I am being tickled!'

51

This was an important lesson for me. As I observe and then interact with these subtle forces in life, so they react and change. Everything changes its behaviour and is modified as it is observed. Thought, I could see, is a language, quite independent of speech.

Over the years I have often had to undo the work of one or two other psychics or mediums who have not truly understood the nature of what they do and who have induced fear and anxiety into the minds of their clients by making negative suggestions or prophesies. My rule is that if I cannot work constructively and creatively with my clients, encouraging and motivating them using the information contained in the light around them, then I should not work with them at all. Sadly, the level of teaching and understanding in this field is generally poor and much harm is done, often unwittingly, in readings and sittings. Recently, I had to undo the nonsense planted in the mind of a young woman by a published author in this field who had told her that she had cracks and tears in her aura. Sheer nonsense, but harmful.

Once, I had to help a woman whose death had been predicted, right to the hour, by a psychic. I supported her and assured her it would not happen as predicted — and it didn't — but, naturally, the fear she lived through had been very damaging.

In my work, I am fortunate in that I meet and work with many different people, from all walks of life and diverse backgrounds — doctors, teachers, poets, singers, housewives, writers, priests, artists, business men and women — many of them quite famous in their own fields.

Early on, I made friends with a female poet, who has had published several collections of her work, and whom I admire greatly. She has always been supportive of my work over the years and I can recall the occasion when we first met. I had been giving a talk to a group in the picturesque town of Lavenham, a few miles from my home. We had been discussing the work I was doing, especially my viewing of auras, and then had broken for tea and cakes.

Heather's aura became very bright as she mingled with the other guests and I felt compelled to observe her. Then I recall seeing a great, powerful light shining close to her, as a man appeared in clergyman's clothes. He was surrounded by young schoolboys and told me that his name on earth had been Peter. He carried a small watering can, the type used for indoor plants, along with a small leather-bound book, rather worn and needing repair. Around this man, were arranged lots of pieces of glass of all descriptions. He smiled at me and as he did so, Heather came across the room towards me for a brief chat. Heather is a very relaxed and warm person and as she approached I felt very comfortable, quite able to ask her if she knew the man I could see, and I described him to her.

She told me she knew who he was. His name had been Peter Spencer, a priest and a teacher (that would explain the schoolboys I had seen) she had known years earlier. As a result of his friendship, she had experienced considerable spiritual unfoldment:

> The last time I saw him was on the 4th November 1972 [my meeting with Heather occurred on 4th November 1985 — the thirteenth anniversary of this date]. I wrote in my diary on that day an extract from J.D. Salinger's *Seymour, An Introduction*. It was a description of Seymour Glass, who always looked for and found God in the strangest places — in ash trays, taxi cab meters, radio announcements, in fact everywhere. I wrote this because it could have been a description of Peter. Before he died three weeks later, I sent him some flowers, but Interflora returned the money because he died before receiving them. With the money I bought a small watering can. The worn leather book needing repair was his prayer book, which his wife gave me and

which I use to this day. This was for me a very amazing and important experience and more than demonstrated Paul's wonderful gift as a sensitive.

For me, this was a landmark in understanding the way in which souls existing in other levels of life can and do make simple communications with us through the personality we remember them as when they lived in this world.

The Death of Pat

One of my greatest teachers was one of my patients from the early days, Pat. Her sister had phoned me. Pat had liver cancer and was not expected to live very long and, in desperation, her sister had found my telephone number and contacted me to see if I could help.

Pat lived in a village a few miles away and as she was unable to travel, I arranged to call one evening. Arriving at the house, I was met by Pat's sister, who showed me into the room where Pat was seated. I remember the image to this day. Pat was a lovely lady, emitting a beautiful blue light all around her. She was uncomplaining and happy despite her illness and was very glad to see me. After speaking to me for a while, she rested her eyes while I placed my hands upon her and allowed the light to move through my fingers and palms, into the beautiful rays of colour around her body. I heard all kinds of beautiful sounds and voices, along with the powerful bell-like ringing I often hear when I am healing.

She seemed to be helped considerably by the session. The residual nagging pain she had felt, despite painkillers, subsided and she smiled as she relaxed into the healing connections we had made together. The blue light around her had deepened and I could perceive a mass of whirling spirals of light, mainly along her spine, but also, in a smaller form, across her body. Pat appeared to me to be supported by a white-blue cloud of energy with many lines travelling across its surface in all kinds of directions, criss-crossing in a network of lights and pulses.

Where the pulses crossed most densely, were the whirling and pulsing ball-like spirals of light, which I now understand to be the chakras. Those along the spinal column and head were the largest, brightest and most intricately coloured — about eight or nine of them it seemed at the time. They radiated on the surface of the body. It was a sea of turning and pulsating centres of light, like a sea of stars clothing dear Pat.

Although I hoped she'd recover physical health (a healer always does), I somehow felt she wouldn't and I left the house, my joy at the renewed optimism the family showed being muted by a deeper sense of what otherwise might be. Caveats from a healer that nothing can ever be promised to a patient in terms of possible physical recovery often go unheeded as one last desperate avenue of hope comes into view.

I saw Pat a few times and she became very peaceful and tranquil but her cancer did not stop growing. She was admitted to hospital where I continued to visit her and help her. One day I called and I saw her apparently asleep, her lighter bodies and true self, hovering a foot or so above her tired, physical shell. I knew she was alive, but it was also clear she only just remained in touch with this world. One of her sons, very tearful, said to me, 'It's all over, isn't it, Paul?' I tried to comfort him and he then left me alone with Pat. Unmistakably, her voice rang out in my head — a strong, yet soft, request. 'Help me move on, Paul,' it said to me.

Glancing across to her face, I could see a light smile on her lips, although her eyes were still closed. Around her, the forms of those friends and family already passed to another dimension waited for her to make her departure to the next plane, and to assist her as she became aware of her greater self and her new plane of being — her new world and next life.

It was now obvious that I could assist her release and, with a sadness in my heart, I directed more of the healing rays to her. A kaleidoscope of energy ran through my fingers and hands and I could see Pat going deeper and deeper into another state.

Soon afterwards she died. The healing she had been given had removed the need for most of her medication as she slipped peacefully away to the higher worlds.

Pat taught me that my work was to help her make her journey. That was her healing and this insight helped me appreciate in later years that it is not for the healer or physician to determine who lives or dies. Such a decision rests within the heart of the patient and only they know how and when they will pass on.

A short time after Pat's death, I gave a lecture to a group of businessmen about the work I was doing and the healing aspect especially. Many were extremely supportive but one or two were very hostile, including a doctor member who, when asked to give a vote of thanks at the end of the session, vehemently attacked what I had said; however, he was later asked to resign from the club as a result. Despite many words of support, I was saddened. At the time, my own uncertainties about my life and abilities resurfaced, as they did from time to time: Was I doing the right thing? Did I need to learn more? and so on. On returning home, a letter had been delivered by hand for me, pushed under the back door. Still crestfallen, I picked it up and opened the envelope. It was a note from Pat's sister, thanking me for all the help I had given during those final days of Pat's life and how she felt my healing work would grow and grow over the years, helping many, many more people. As I read these words, I could see Pat's face.

The note went on to say how she had felt compelled to write it and that she was sure she sensed Pat around her, giving her approval. This was just the tonic I needed and I was happy to take it as welcome encouragement from a dear friend in another dimension.

Colours

As a guest on a radio show in the USA recently, the expression 'strike me pink' came up in conversation with the programme's host. Some years ago, she had a neighbour who was English who used the expression, and she felt it was a very 'Brit' way to speak.

As I was discussing and reading aura colours live on air, it was interesting to note how often we 'colour' our language to give it meaning.

When sad, we have 'the blues', we can also become 'green with envy', enjoy 'purple patches', grow 'red with anger' and feel 'in the pink'. Cowards are often referred to as having a 'yellow streak'. These references have a particular relevance to the esoteric or other meanings that can be attributed to the coloured light of the astral and mental bodies of the auric fields. However, it is important to realise that the interpretation of colour in an aura is a complex and sophisticated process, requiring some years of study and practice. Perceiving the colours is fairly easy. Understanding and interpreting them takes a while and to say that blue means this, red means that and so on throughout the spectrum and beyond is a little like saying a clear blue sky means that there are no clouds. That may be true, but only part of the story.

The rays and their colours indicate certain attributes and qualities, or their absence, and sometimes subtle changes or differences can alter the meaning quite considerably. In the range of yellows, for example, one can see everything from selfish, intellectual ambition to an elevated, altruistic clear and open mind. It is also important to look at the relationship between colours, how much there is visible and where it is positioned, along with its relation to the other bodies, especially the physical.

Texture, smoothness and density in auric colours also have considerable importance, so the following guide to the rays and their colours is very much a general introduction and should be treated as such. It cannot replace good teaching and ongoing study and observation, which I consider the keys to my work. Even though life has always been a mass of colour for me, and remains so, and, given a name or even a general identity, I can see an aura, a chakra network and hear thought patterns in operation through what I regard as my second nature, I am nevertheless continually in a state of learning and research — the eternal student. The vast and inspiring world that such study and commitment can open for you will be well worth the hard work.

The butterfly and the rainbow
Exercise 8

In my workshops, I often use the butterfly and the rainbow as a way of connecting with colours, the voice within them and what they have to say to us.

Just as you and I are living, complex and marvellous blends of universal and cosmic light and intelligence, rays, too, are living entities. We can learn to communicate with them and the angelic presence within them.

1. Sit quietly, where you will not be disturbed. Use Exercise 4 to clear your aura and radiate.
2. Relax and close your eyes. Imagine yourself outdoors on a sunny, early summer's day. A gentle rain shower is falling over the beautiful scene before your eyes — a green, fresh meadow surrounded by tall trees, all basking in bright golden sunlight.

3. A small, lone cloud floats away into the distance, scattering the last drops of moisture onto the countryside below. Everything is moist, full of promise and vitality and exquisite perfumes rise up from the wild flowers in view everywhere.

4. Watch and see, as a beautiful rainbow forms in the sky above you. It is vivid and powerful, clear and vibrant! The colours in the rainbow call you. You wish to be amongst them, you wish to touch them, to hear them, to bathe in them.

5. A small butterfly caresses the stamen of a nearby flower. You watch the butterfly and then join it on your journey of discovery as it rises with you up into the air, supported by the warm breeze. Imagine yourself as you fly up, up, to the rainbow, through these wonderful colours. Enjoy it a while.

6. As you soak in the colours, let each one dance with you in a magical dancing whirl. Let it impress its nature on you: red, orange, yellow, green, blue, indigo, violet; purple, silver, gold; all the colours.

7. In each colour, you feel safe, happy and alert. In each colour, an angel appears, a beautiful glowing being. Listen to it. It will speak to you and communicate the hidden messages within its colour. Explore and enjoy these moments.

8. Fly through your rainbow once more, and then, gently, return to the earth, to the spot where you stood earlier. Look up at the rainbow again and then across to your butterfly. Say a thank you.

9. Fill yourself with light and radiate that light while you connect again with the earth. Open your eyes slowly and return to normal awareness.

Repeat the exercise often and note what you are learning. It is a long and beautiful journey and gives life and the universe a special way to speak to you!

Meanings

Spirit and thought

We commence our analysis of the rays by considering the colours from the top of the spectrum and some of the meanings they convey to us. As we make our way through the colours, it is a good idea to use some colouring pencils to create small swatches or draw circles of each one as we explore them.

This analysis will help your general colour awareness and encourage the development of your rapport with the energy and light of each ray, in each of its subtle variations. It will also be useful as your first 'colour chart', which you can refer to as your research progresses.

It is important to note that we all have all colours in our aura — we have the potential to be anything we choose. What shapes our human nature is what we reveal of ourselves — in other words, what 'light' we show to others through our thoughts and actions.

Indigo

Indigo is the ray of integration of the physical, mental and emotional within the individual. It is a very special ray having strong links with the pituitary gland in the physical body.

When indigo is seen, this ray often indicates sincerity and selflessness in thinking. It usually facilitates detachment and fine spirituality, producing very high motivation, and is evidence that mastery of the physical nature and its reintegration with the soul and spirit has begun to some degree. It is the ray that links the conscious and unconscious aspects of the mind.

Those who show a fair amount of indigo in their auric and chakra systems are usually very influential, simply by their presence; they have to say very little and embody true charisma. Indigo is relatively rare.

Second sight, without any evidence of specific accompanying psychic manifestation or ability, is common.

I saw this ray in profusion recently in the aura of a wonderful senior nurse who was managing a very difficult situation in a hospital with great skill and wisdom.

Violet

Violet also gives us a colour range associated with a high spirituality. It frequently, though not always, links with clairvoyant capacities, and usually these are discarded or subjugated to higher needs rather than being used in a psychic manner.

Violet produces a sense of the unity of all things in individuals, a feeling of connectedness and prayerfulness, that of the deep profound prayer that borders on contemplation. Usually, this ray predisposes its possessor to an extremely fine intuition (not psychism, which is altogether different and of a lower order).

Bright violets are not as common in auras as people often think, and are usually darkened with blue, indicating over-sensitivity and intermittent depressive modes. A grape-like violet can produce the kind of neurotic psychic who is rather negative and insecure and who has to be handled with 'kid gloves' by others.

The true bright violets bring the higher frequencies and characteristics to the fore, and link to the imagination, especially when there is evidence of bright blues and turquoise in the same auric field.

Purple

Purple is a colour that is fairly easy to find in most auras and chakras. It denotes psychic ability and mediumistic gifts. It can produce a fairly compassionate and sensitive individual at best. At worst, it tends to produce in us the desire for status, and a strong personal will. This is evident often in a selfish, aggressive individualism, where the, apparently, strongest get to the top.

It is a colour not necessarily indicative of high spiritual values or understanding — true of many clairvoyants who have this ray and who are often unwisely revered and relied on by those who follow them. Purple is commonly seen in mediums, especially those with theatrical delusions and a desire for fame.

Amethyst

I once watched a beautiful woman giving a lecture on the work of Dr Rudolph Steiner. She was obviously inspired and I found her talk most moving and informative. As she spoke, I was also completely in awe of the incredibly vibrant, translucent amethyst light that glowed around her head. I can see it clearly to this day. It was breathtaking. She was indeed an old and very wise soul.

Fifteen years ago I would have described amethyst as rare when I viewed it in an aura, but now I know it to be increasingly evident. It seems at this important time, more and more people are revealing their amethyst light, the ray indicative of a very special being or a special quality within the individual.

It reveals a great capacity for prayer, contemplation and high aspiration. Amethyst helps us to be aware of the higher planes of life that link us with our soul and spiritual selves and beyond. It enables us to link effectively with other dimensions. Nearly always seen around the top of the aura (as are the other purples and violets), it is the colour of the old soul who has come here for this lifetime on the earth to serve, and who may well have to wait until the latter half of the incarnation to unfold their true purpose.

A common phenomenon for old souls is the sense of *déjà vu* that sometimes affects them; those moments when we sudden- ly sense a momentary detachment, recognising and knowing a particular instant, almost as if taking part in an action replay, a feeling of 'I've seen this before — although I couldn't have done!' Sometimes the *déjà vu* takes on a deeper, more powerful significance, linking us with an earlier incarnation on the earth when we find ourselves in a new location, city or town, yet we are strangely familiar with it. Or it reminds us we have had visions of the future.

To reveal a large area of amethyst shows a wonderful being; a true spiritual leader or teacher on earth will display this ray clearly, unless he or she is an avatar, when gold will predominate.

Famous people can have surprisingly 'routine' colour patterns, except in the yellow rays, and perhaps purple, where there is often a suggestion of ambition, sometimes ruthlessness.

Reflections and colour consciousness

Before moving on to the next segment of colour analysis, take some time to reflect on the wonder of colour.

You may have books on interior design or decorating, the works of great painters, or even a catalogue of summer garden flowers, to hand. Look through them, enjoy the colours and be conscious of how the colours effect you. With the paintings in particular, look at the way in which the artists have used colours and made certain juxtapositions. Observe how the colours affect each other and how you view them. Study the complementary colours, reds and greens, blues and oranges, yellows and purples or violets, and see how they contrast. Consider your own choices of colour for your clothing, house furnishings and so on. Think deeply about colour and develop a new, more conscious rapport with this vibrational world.

When you have the opportunity, visit a gallery. Look at all the paintings and especially the work of the Impressionists, along with some modern works such as Braque, Picasso, Kandinsky and Paul Klee. Study Van Gogh's use of colour and how he described form with his brush strokes of flaming hues. And also the wonderful pieces by Cézanne.

Look at the flowers in your garden; visit bluebell woods in the spring. The vibration of flowers is very high and is close to that of the aura.

Use some crayons, coloured pencils, paints or whatever you can find and simply enjoy yourself making coloured patterns for fun. Allow the child in you to play again as it once did. This will foster a bright new relationship with colour and will support your research here in this world of subtle light.

Ideas, ideals and intuition

Blue

Although intuition is a feature of several of the rays — violets, greens and silver — it has a concrete connection with all the blue rays, especially the lighter blues and the turquoise end of the grouping. Just as the highest aspect of the violet ray stimulates the imagination in the pineal gland at the behest of our spirit, the blues have a function in funnelling the ideas of the intuitive mind, which the imagination has formed, towards the more practical aspects of the yellow rays.

Blue people, with bright blues, are the idealists of our race, those who aspire and are devoted in life in some way — the carers, teachers and ideas men and women; these are very creative rays. When our minds are in the 'open' phase, we are at our most creative, and very receptive to ideas percolating down to us. Some we can understand, usually in picture form, others through a more subtle sense of direction or inspiration that touches us and makes the heart leap with optimism. The light blues are also the 'Micawber' rays, those of the optimist who believes something better is always possible or that 'something will turn up'.

Blues also have connections with the ears and throat and are closely associated with sound and communication — often evident in musicians, media workers, journalists; they are also linked with intuitive and 'mental dialogue' as well as the spoken word.

Light, violet blue

This is a glorious hue, highly spiritual, and relates to a soul of very high aspiration, one who seeks the truth. There were hints of this colour visible in Mother Teresa's aura, the colour of real saintliness and individuals who are possessed by a genuine sense of divinity. When connected with amethyst, we see a powerful individual who can help shape or influence the lives of many for the good. As well as the better known saints, I have also seen this in the aura of some apparently ordinary and humble individuals, who use their influence in more subtle ways. It is relatively rare.

Turquoise

The ray of the exceptionally creative, usually very perceptive and extremely idealistic, individual, who is relatively easily hurt or disappointed because of a tendency to put others on a pedestal. These souls are usually highly sensitive, and can be very loyal, with a conscience that will nag them.

Those with turquoise are generally very observant and perceptive and fairly fast in forming concepts. A mercurial ray, this is for those who sometimes like fast-moving lives and variety of experience and who don't like getting 'bogged down'.

Sky blue

Sky blue is another idealistic ray and, like turquoise, very intuitive, often the ray of the teacher and sometimes those who like mystical approaches to life — poets like Blake had this in profusion. These people are frequently inspired and often have a facility to calm others and sometimes themselves.

This ray provides an openness to ideas. Artists, writers and musicians sometimes worry that they have no ideas. This is never true. We all have ideas all the time but the intellect sometimes reasons them away and this can create the dearth of ideas that we might feel at any time. Ideas usually flow, like teardrops, through this colour, waiting to burst into concrete-thought existence.

Generally this ray's attributes are honesty, caring and good voice powers (for example, singing). Sky blue is a good ray for the development of self-discipline and for those who pray for others, especially their healing.

Royal and mid-blues; deep blue-blacks

Royal blue and the other mid-blues are often the indicator of one who has a religious approach to life, who likes their spiritual life to have quite clearly defined structures and patterns. In esoteric terms, they are the rays of the white magician, with a love for and even a predisposition to ritual, and those spiritual highs, known as Siddhis in the East. I once observed this in a Catholic bishop, who, I understood from a Catholic monsignor who knew him well, was truly a man of prayer and one who lay great store by the ritual of the church.

However, heavy areas of these mid-blues and their darker cousins, the deep blue-blacks can lead quite literally to 'the blues' — an overwhelmed, depressed, over-calm state, bordering on inertia. It is interesting how often someone who loses their job or career position sees their blue ray darken: they often still have ideas, once the initial shock has subsided, and sometimes too many ideas come through, but they may become increasingly casual, inert and unable to act — sometimes much talking but little action. In such cases, it can be clear that the lighter blues show long strands of blue-black in them, once again imprisoning the ideas of the individual in a heavy, negative state. Like the violets, the capacity to think creatively in the blue rays can be turned into destructive channels, when thinking becomes laced with negative emotions and fear. The contemplative need evident in mid-blue can lead to too much isolation, and the melancholia of the hermit as the blue darkens.

An interest in magic for more selfish reasons, mindless idolatry, fanaticism and a tendency to bigotry link with this darker end of the blue ray. From a spiritual or esoteric point of view, this ray, when consistently evident in individual auras, forms an individual who likes 'proof', visible miracles and spiritual phenomena — 'evidence' of the spiritual life. It is a low and depressing vibration, thankfully not often seen in large quantities.

Growth and balance

Green

The splendour of the green light and the potential range of its interpretation is remarkable. Psychological experimentation where deprivation from greens was introduced brought to the surface very powerful neuroses and lethargy. It is the colour synonymous with growth, balance and change, and I am always most interested when I see vibrant emeralds dominating an auric field, for it is telling me that the individual concerned is almost certainly in a phase of life where much adaptability, possibly to profound change, is required and evident.

The lighter greens show generosity and kindness and true affluence, not the type necessarily connected with financial wealth; rather, the affluence of people who are comfortable with life.

Yellow- and apple-green

These colours are generally indicative of a balanced, highly creative tendency or nature, often very intuitive in the true sense. These are big hearted people with a real 'feel' for life, a positive attitude with a refined and loving emotional nature — the high emotions.

Where there is much yellow-green, we meet a philosophical mind, usually someone who is very adaptable and who can see both sides of the story. When matched with a pink-peach shade, we have a genuine peacemaker, the best ambassador we could ever meet. I once knew a head teacher who had a little of this ray and was greatly loved and respected by pupils, teachers and parents alike. He was always able to see both sides of any argument, always sensing a solution somewhere. I can never remember him showing dislike for anyone, even the most challenging of individuals. Joy tends to spring from the heart of those who have evolved and developed this beautiful resonance in their higher bodies.

Emerald

Emeralds are perhaps the most common of the green rays. Again, they show adaptability — the lighter the colour, the more flexible the individual — and when linked with turquoise and lighter blues they bring openness and honesty.

Light emerald shows relative balance at the mental and emotional level, along with growth, and the vitality that accompanies a youthful desire to discover, acquire new skills and generally improve.

It is linked with those optimists who seek good in others and in life, accepting change as inevitable and using opportunities positively rather than always finding a horde of insuperable problems. There is always space for true love in the lighter emeralds, the love that expects no return.

As the ray darkens to reveal mid-emerald, we still see the potential for growth and a degree of willingness to change and go with the flow — here we meet true affluence again. This is also a colour synonymous with mental vitality, but if the colour shows too deep a hue, it can imply a tendency towards rash or even impulsive, if well-intentioned, behaviour, and sometimes an over-emotionalism. This was very evident during mourning after the death of Princess Diana, where amidst much genuine, heartfelt grief, there were almost unpleasant releases of highly charged emotional energy. This colour can be very dangerous when coupled with the deeper blues in an aura, leading to intolerance of anyone who doesn't seem to feel as you do, or display the same zeal or passion for an idea.

Olive green

Where the olive greens appear, and we all have some somewhere (I have yet to view an aura completely devoid of it), we touch some of our weaker aspects of emotional fragility, seeing a tendency towards tantrums and childish, sulky behaviour, and also meanness, or lack of charity. Deep olive, which has much black in it, is really the green of envy and this colour vividly pulses in moments where its channel or owner is trying to be deceitful. This is very commonly seen in states of paranoid behaviour, and in addicts of various kinds. It is, not surprisingly some may think, commonly activated in the emotional bodies of those in politics, both local and national, as the lower greens can be associated with manipulative, emotional energy (Hitler used this energy to devastating effect). Manipulative people tend to want everyone else to change to suit them, but are often unwilling to effect change within themselves — the antithesis of the lighter green rays.

The concrete mind and the intellect

Yellow

Recently, whilst giving a series of consultations in northwest Germany, I was visited by a female psychologist of some repute. She specialises in working with those who, in adult life, are trying to come to terms with physical, mental and emotional abuses that they have suffered earlier in their lives. She has a fine reputation and is extremely skilled in her work. I was not surprised therefore, to see a relatively large expanse of the two highest yellow rays — the light, gold-white yellow and pale primrose revealing a fine and potentially wonderful mind. The white-gold yellow is still rare to see, and I have seldom viewed such an expanse as in Maria's aura. She has the highly positioned, spiritual mind that can work closely with her intuition. For this to be at all possible, the individual has to have established a deepening link with the soul and is moving towards enlightenment. When the gold ray is also visible in the same space in such an aura, then we really are in the presence of someone special.

The pale primrose, which blended into the gold-yellow of Maria's aura, gave her a clear, bright intellect that was largely unselfish and bulging with knowledge, talent and potential.

The yellows are the rays of the intellect and are common amongst scientists, mathematicians, accountants and those who love analysis and exploring theoretical minutiae. Mid-yellow particularly shows a capacity for sound, analytical thinking and the ability to deal logically with concrete ideas. Those good at assessment and calculation, in their element creating structures and theories, usually have a smooth, clear mid-yellow in some quantity radiating around their head. Too much of this ray can produce a logical mind that can't believe in anything it can't prove through a mathematical approach — it needs a theorem for everything and can lead to a reductionistic and spiritually barren mind. The 'boffin' can sometimes reveal much of the deep orange-yellows, leading to intellectual snobbery and even arrogance. Much of our culture and science has been blighted by an excess of this ray and a lack of its more intuitive cousins — the light blue rays. As a result we live in very much a left-brain world dominated by the deep yellows, where lateral, creative thinking is still relatively rare and new ideas are often scorned, but later prove to be useful and viable.

Too much deep yellow produces an over-intellectual individual, who tends to use his or her mental prowess selfishly. The intellect knows the car is a brilliant piece of technology, but without interaction with intuition, it fails to foresee the pollution and ill health its over-use can bring to our society.

Some, like me, suffer from inadequate deeper yellow, and have a problem 'grounding' their many ideas and putting them into action. Yellow is vital in realising plans. A balanced psyche relies on a good exchange between the inspired ideas and lateral thinking of the blues and images of the violets, given shape and reality through a practical, logical yellow.

Occasionally, the yellow light has a burnt-like effect either in spots on its surface or around the edge of the ray's field in the aura. This indicates arrogance and a ruthlessness in the individual in seeing through their own plans and personal desires — an unsavoury type who likes to control and manipulate others. Yellow that is heavily conditioned by orange can produce the most overwhelming people, who flatten all before them in their insensitive pursuit of their own opinions and objectives; they are often psychological bullies.

On a more positive note, the lighter yellows are good for clear thought and meditation and useful when visualised before tests and examinations where sound memory is required. And there is a link here with the tradition of tying yellow ribbons round old oak trees to remember those held hostage or in prison lest we forget them.

My work is based on my experience and what my vision has taught me over the years. Trust your own experience and vision and follow the model that works for you. If your colour chart reveals different things to you, then go with it and use it. However, I find that there is a general consensus among good clairvoyants in relation to many of the rays and their meanings, and those who have studied with me usually find my evaluations and models work for them too.

Physical, material and other aspects

Vermilion

When my mother was dying from bone cancer, I sat with her in the bedroom of her little house as she slipped in and out of consciousness. I could see the way the higher bodies were moving upwards gradually away from her tired, physical shell and I knew that her transition was near. I was also aware that I could see little evidence, if any, of vermilion red in the aura around her.

The doctor called to see how things were, as we waited attentively. He said that in his opinion she would not pass for a couple of days and, in my tired state, I rather allowed his assessment to override what I could see, for it is the disappearance of the vermilion ray that signals death as being imminent.

It had been an exhausting day, both physically and emotionally, and we decided to accept the doctor's advice and return home to look after the children until morning. On our arrival at our house, some half an hour or so later, the message had already been received that, soon after my wife, Sue, and I had left, my mother had passed into the higher life.

I should really have trusted my own judgement, for it had shown clearly the ray that governs our physical incarnation and our 'will-to-be' was almost gone. Perhaps I was subconsciously guided to leave for reasons that some higher purpose understood, but this ray is vital as it literally keeps us earthed, grounded, here on the planet.

A balanced proportion of the vermilion ray is the sign of a well-balanced and down-to-earth individual, who has good physical strength. Along with orange rays, it reveals sexual drive, too much orange indicating an oversexed and even promiscuous individual. It is the 'will-to-be-incarnate' and is the vibration that brings us into our physical lives at birth. Good reliable clairvoyance of the aura would make some 'life or death' decisions easier, perhaps, as it can be quite clear when an individual no longer wishes to remain incarnate, despite our attempts to keep them here at all costs and often enough with the aid of questionable medical technologies. When the vermilion ray has gone, nothing will keep an individual alive on earth.

Deep red
Deep reds are often visible in the developing auras of young people, assisting physical growth, which is actually quite stressful in many ways, especially during adolescent years when youngsters literally 'shoot up' like new spring flowers, as my 14-year-old son has recently done. These reds moving towards crimson illustrate this kind of growth and also the drive that comes with youth and youthful, enthusiastic attitudes.

Sometimes black creeps into the red, giving us a black-red. Though this tends to be visible in all our auras from time to time, it is more noticable at times of frustration and anger and in the ridge or bar formation visible during depression, particularly chronic, mental collapse. This red, especially as it becomes more aubergine in colour, shows passion, and sensuality in profusion. When seen with lots of vermilion and bright orange, it can create enormous sexual and relationship problems. One woman I saw recently was in terrible despair because of her inability to control her sexual appetites; the colour of the ray I saw confirmed this clearly.

Such energy, along with the orange ray, has to be transmuted to some extent through the chakras of the heart and throat, leading us to be more creative at higher, mental levels and ensuring our relationships are formed as much as possible around loving and sharing, rather than desire. This is the real reason for celibacy — the need to transmute and use physical energies and forces for higher spiritual experience.

Rose-pink

Rose-pink is wonderful evidence of the powerful and significant transmutation that has already taken place in us. It is the red of individual will, raised through the heart, so we become less self-centred and more aware of others. Rose is the colour of true, real affection and love. It is indicative of our desire being transmuted into love with great compassion, to 'feel' for others and to also have the desire to do whatever we can to bring healing into their lives.

However, when the rose becomes too pink, it does tend to dilute its effectiveness. A lot of pink can produce nice enough people, but they are often a little passive as well as sympathetic. Individuals with a lot of pink may share your sorrow, but may be ineffective when it comes to the practical side of things, especially when you need to find solutions. In such souls, empathy and its consequent compassion has drifted into sympathy.

Orange

Orange rays are generally indicative of the state of physical vitality and energy in an individual. Inextricably linked with the reds in their action, they give us the energy or power for physical health. The reds, especially vermilion, show the strength of will to focus our energy. Too much will, but not enough energy leads to exhaustion, too much energy not directed properly will lead to a dissipation and lack of focus, common in some young people. This is why managed exercise like yoga and the martial arts, where the two properties are integrated effectively, are so valuable and necessary. My many years as a practitioner of Tae Kwon Do were of great value to me and the fact that my busy life makes it no longer possible to attend my club is a sadness to me at times.

A strong clear orange tells of a good capacity for healing in the individual's energy body. It also indicates a healthy sexual capacity and can promote a powerful personality. However, too much orange can make us overpowering.

Clear orange is important in giving us the power and energy to pursue our ambitions by being active and taking steps to give birth to our ideas in practical ways.

Orange-red

Where orange-red is seen, we notice a tendency in the individual to overreact, especially when the area of orange light apparent in the aura has a brownish halo around the edges. I recall one professional footballer who possessed outstanding skill but never truly realised much of his potential because of this tendency. His orange ray is very red in places and it is framed in a deep ochre colour which leads to the explosion of uncontrolled energy and emotion, consequently blighting his career and personal life.

Where orange-reds are visible in the auras of older people, and where physical vitality has ebbed away significantly, anxiety that is persistent and extremely disabling is found. In an individual who is in receipt of healing or has some significant healing already active within his or her physical body, patches of orange are clearly evident in the area concerned. However, where the situation or the pathology is well established and may be causing concern, some deep reds will be visible, along with black-browns if the condition is serious and in need of considerable therapeutic work and healing.

Brown

The browns are generally indicative of lowered energy and vitality, and sometimes pain, although only when interacting with black. Generally speaking, the darker the brown, the worse the energy condition in that part of the aura. Muddy green-browns are usually common where there is poor health, with pathological problems and maybe also mental troubles indicated if in the top half of the field. A bright red–orange–brown is often a sign of healing taking place in heavily diseased tissue.

Khaki brown

I have often observed a particular khaki brown in the aura of those who have been physically abused in some manner, again, usually with large areas of black interacting with it. A pale khaki is usually visible where there is serious morbidity in body tissue.

Golden brown

When an individual is dying very peacefully, around the physical body, along with many other beautiful colours, one can see a kind of golden brown radiating close to its surface. This usually sparkling ray is showing us that the individual is 'letting go' or relinquishing his or her physical life and self with a calm dignity and is ready to move on.

Black

I think it is important to say that black appears in almost every aura I have observed and studied, and that now runs into many thousands. I cannot recall ever perceiving it to be totally absent. After a lecture I had given some years ago, a woman approached me with great trepidation and confessed that an 'aura reader' at a psychic fayre had told her she had 'a big chunk of black' at the bottom of her aura and she must free herself of it immediately if it was not to cause her problems.

What the 'aura reader' had failed to understand was that she too must have a comparable vibration of the black in her auric space, otherwise she would not have been able to recognise it in another. We can only recognise in others that which is part of our experience. Whilst it is true that black is evidence of times we have been 'in the dark' in our own lives — the pain and suffering we have all had at sometime, if not in this lifetime, then in another — it was a foolish statement from someone who seemed the embodiment of the maxim 'a little knowledge is a dangerous thing.' I was able to reassure the woman that she was not alone and that through prayer and meditation and constructive attitudes she would gradually transmute much of her dark experience and her 'blackness', retaining just enough in the mental body to help her understand the darkness others experience. We remember or record everything we experience in our lives and forget nothing.

Higher levels

Of the other rays that have a correspondence in our own spectrum of colour, gold and silver must be mentioned. Golds and silvers were common around the angelic entities I used to see in my childhood at Mass (and still do see) and are often evident in auras, usually in small quantities.

Gold

Generally speaking, gold rays are indicative of wisdom, and a great soul will reveal much gold. A true Initiate, one who has overcome their physical nature and who you or I might describe as perfect, would have a white-gold auric field. This reveals to us that they have worked the ultimate alchemy and turned the lower base colours into a radiant golden light.

Jesus Christ would have radiated such a light, as would Buddha and other great incarnated souls. When this colour is evident in an aura, it is usually demonstrating that the individual has recently or will shortly experience a significant and important change in their lives and that they will have the wisdom to work through it perfectly. As we get older, we often feel the need for more gold around us in our everyday lives — a subconscious yearning perhaps for others to see the wisdom in us that should accompany passing years. We all wish we had a Midas touch of some kind.

Silver

Silver is wonderful. It is also giving us a message — it is the ray of higher intuition, compelling us to follow the powerful insights and guidance coming to us from our spiritual self or soul.

A dear friend suddenly felt a deep and sustained urge to move on and completely change her life's direction. Everyone around her thought she was experiencing some kind of emotional collapse and mental breakdown, as she seemed to be throwing away all she had worked so hard to achieve. However, she followed her heart and worked creatively and began a new life which eventually proved to be a perfect decision. The silver vibration in her aura gave her both the desire and courage to follow what was clearly important in the unfolding of her destiny, even though initially it was not the obvious and comfortable thing to do.

The silver ray connects with the love of God in us and the consequential desire in us to do God's will and follow the path we came here to follow. It summons up in us the trust or faith we need to walk the intuitive road and serve life through our own efforts, joyfully, however difficult that may be at times. The angels work with us via the silver ray, and help us to walk our pathway, observing as we go the meaningful coincidences we encounter (what Carl Jung termed 'synchronicity').

Incoming Rays

It is appropriate to mention here another visual phenomenon concerning the coloured rays and the auric oval forms we can see. Around every aura, bands of light can be seen. They reveal their deepest hue closest to the mental body (see Plate 5).

I have learned that this is indicative of an exchange of vibrations taking place between the collective mental body or mind of the universe, and that of the individual. These rays, forming bands, appear to be somehow tucked in behind the oval body form, as they filter into the equivalent mental vibration or colour, showing how we can draw on different levels of collective or universal mental energy in order to express our individual thinking and mental processes.

The rays are nearly always clear and smooth in form and line and should not be confused with the thought rays or the cords that link individuals, which, in contrast, are usually multi-coloured and snake off into the distance, bending and twisting as they go.

In Renaissance painting in particular, rays of light in halo effect around an individual, whether it be Jesus, or a saint, were frequently shown to stress the specialness and holiness of the subject. When we have all evolved and attained true mastery of ourselves and have overcome our lower natures, we too will inspire paintings of golden auras depicting the wise interaction, within those broad golden radiations, of our minds with the divine cosmic mind — the ultimate human unfoldment.

Some Colour Distributions

There are as many visible patterns and arrangements of colour in emotional or astral and mental auras as there are individuals. And the pattern within the aura of each individual changes, moment by moment, day by day.

A sudden alarm bell will bring a surge of reds and oranges upward across the front of the aura, but eventually, this subsides to reveal the underlying, more slowly evolving pattern that was visible beforehand. Every experience changes us, but usually in a gradual, piece by piece manner.

Disease

Someone experiencing a diseased state in their physical body will show particular colour mixes close to the seat of the problem. In relatively mild conditions which may eventually be healed, there are usually pulsing areas of orange visible and the hue of the orange is quite intense and deep — the more the observer focuses attention on it, the more intense it seems to become.

Where the condition is chronic, the orange will be surrounded by a deep red. The deeper and blacker the red, the more chronic the condition in the physical body. If the observer is also able to see the etheric body, a corresponding lack of lustre in that body will also be evident, where the hair-like strands lie flattened on the surface.

I had a patient who I had known for many years. She had been told that a lump that had formed in her breast was 'suspicious' and may have been cancerous or pre-cancerous. Surgery was suggested but she had decided that she did not wish to follow that path, preferring to use a variety of complementary methods and approaches, including some healing and counselling from me.

Although I always suggest to my patients that they respect the orthodox ways, especially from a diagnostic point of view, I must admit to being puzzled by what she had been told. In the rays of her astral and mental bodies, I could see an indication of tissue change, but not the muddy grey-brown and black that I expected to see, usually associated with cancerous tissue. These colours, and orange, fringed with deepening reds and black-browns, muddy grey-greens or pale khaki brown are seen where there is a high level of pathological damage or distress in the physical body, depending on the type of tissue change occurring.

Later on, further tests and treatments suggested that the tissue was not cancerous and the surgery would have been unnecessary. I was delighted my perception had proved correct.

I have met many psychics and intuitives who claim they are able to give medical diagnoses. I don't doubt that many can and do make useful diagnoses. I have done this myself many·times, even sometimes by proxy, where I have been able to see the aura and energy field of a friend or relative of the person who is consulting me and have noticed a condition needing urgent help.

On one occasion, it concerned the brother of a client who showed cancer in his aura, although he was unaware of it at the time. An immediate test revealed the disease and he was able to receive treatment. Another noteworthy experience that comes to mind was the husband of a female client. I could see he was having difficulty in the tissues around his spine and that appropriate massage and gentle manipulation would free him of the pain and disablement he was suffering. His doctor had offered no suggestion other than bed-rest and painkillers. I recommended my client tried to get her husband to a very good osteopath I knew at the time. This she did, and the healing he subsequently experienced was so remarkable that the osteopath called me to express his astonishment at my diagnosis and also at how dramatic the improvement was in just one consultation. He couldn't fathom it at all and, although we knew each other well, the osteopath remained puzzled as to how I could make a diagnosis on someone I had never met.

Please note that no intuitive or diagnostic psychic is ever infallible. Not only the intuitive but all safe and appropriate forms of diagnosis should be used at all times.

A General Aura Picture

While we are all different and no two auras are exactly the same, there is a general pattern to the distribution of auric colours as perceived in the emotional and mental bodies.

We noted in Chapter 1 that, though the astral field is a more dense and volatile echo of the mental aura and body, with certain colour correspondences in both, the colours in the mental body are finer and more 'metallic' in their radiance and move and pulse at a much slower rate and in a more flowing manner.

In simple terms, we 'look through' the astral rays and, understanding that the two levels of auric body are closely connected, we can use what we see in the astral plane to help us to see through to the mental level, rather like looking through a window from one level to the next (see Plate 6).

Generally, in an auric field, certain colour distributions predominate. The reds, oranges and some darker greens tend to gravitate to the bottom of the aura, with the red nearest to the feet. Orange is very mobile and will take extra physical forces to the top half of the body if, and when, it is needed for any reason — exercise, disease, healing, for example. The reds will also rise up quickly in some people, particularly with aubergine and black specks in them; for example, in the case of rising passions or sudden bursts of aggression, or anger, or the need for quick action and determined application to a task, such as helping in an accident or facing aggression.

The yellow ray in our current evolutionary stage, is often in the top half of the aura, frequently around the head. This is because of the emphasis on intellectual prowess and development in our society and culture.

The mid- and lighter-green rays frequently settle around the centre of the body, as does the rose ray (a transmuted or elevated vermilion), moving upwards in moments of great change and down again as the change is either completed, or in some cases, temporarily avoided! However, when matters concerning the heart and love and affection dominate, in a pleasant fashion at least, we can literally be 'in the pink' and it is an interesting fact that a slight embarrassment, especially concerning matters of the heart, can show themselves in blushes and a rush of pink in the auric field, especially to the head area. A powerful surge will mask the yellow and produce temporary confusion. Those in the full flush of romance find it difficult to think about anything else on these occasions.

The lighter blues will frequently rest higher in the aura than the deeper and mid-blues. However, a fringe or border of dark or deep blue around the lighter blues can signal a kind of lethargic, melancholic state — 'the blues' — especially if it contains a little black.

Violets, purples and magentas also gravitate towards the top of the auric field and are at their most dynamic in that space. When they slip below the waist level, we can experience a complete lack of imaginative ideas and also a feeling of oversensitivity and an overemotional tendency, echoed sometimes in digestive disruptions in the stomach, but more often the colon and bowel. This can sometimes be the effect of our dreams being destroyed.

Sometimes we hear descriptions such as 'he has a blue aura,' or 'her aura is green.' While temporarily we can experience mental and emotional changes that will seem to show a dominance of one colour or another, this is simply an indication that the normally brief and always transient appearance of one particular ray is masking most or all the other rays, producing an illusory effect. But the good clairvoyant will still see the other rays, albeit briefly overlaid by this dominant ray and its colour. This kind of activity reflects those experiences, maybe a thought, feeling or mood, that sometimes briefly dominate or overwhelm us, but which then subside and fade away.

'Typical' Auric Patterns

Though of course there are no clearly definable, 'typical' auric patterns, and every aura is unique and different, you will find that some colour distributions are revealed more often than others. Plate 7 illustrates a 'typical' colour distribution in this sense. There are also some interesting types to be aware of.

The intellectual

Those of a strong, left-brain predominance, who find their intellectual capacities rule, and tend to like and prefer logical, linear modes of working, often have considerable large, smooth areas of yellow in the top half of their auric fields. The yellow is often hard-edged and quite even.

Such a structure produces our accountants, lawyers and reductionist scientists. Too much mid-yellow leaves us with the rationalist — if he can't see it and touch it, then it doesn't exist. Such a soul will always want proof. Often there is a corresponding inadequacy of the intuitive, creative blues to help these individuals think openly, laterally and creatively, and sometimes, violets and purples are absent altogether, concealed in the depths of the auric field.

Where the yellow tends to be fringed with a burnt orange-yellow, an intellectual arrogance is often evident. Such people have closed minds and often eventually meet with a crisis that awakens them to a broader view of life.

The artistic individual

In creative, people, those visually alive individuals who love colour and often enjoy artistic pursuits, we see vast areas of violets and purples. If the spread of the colours is too great, with a little of the pale blues visible, the individual can be oversensitive, a little impractical and yet quite visionary.

Some artistic individuals tend to link to other dimensions quite easily and then mentally interact and fantasise, becoming depressive. This can be observed when the auric colours start to show a deep grape-violet edge, especially around the top of the aura. The individual is trapped by his or her own imagination and can adopt an almost autistic appearance at times.

On the positive side, smooth violets produce high creative imagination which, with sufficient mid-yellows, reveal highly

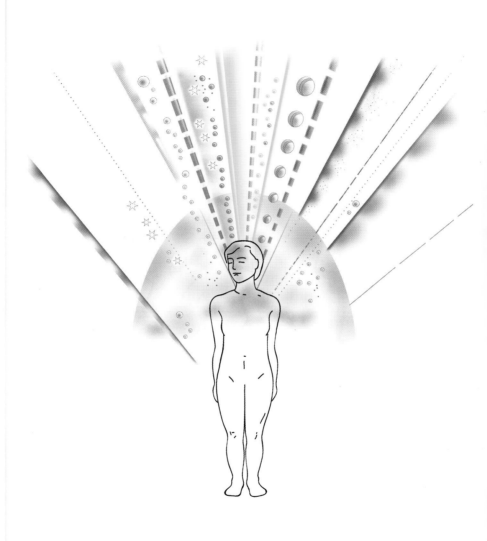

Plate 1   Streams of aspirational and inspirational light.

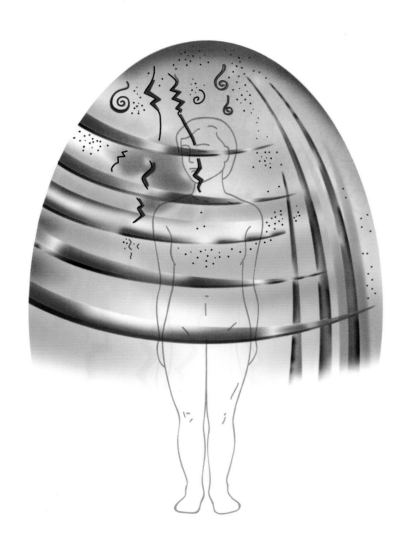

Plate 4 Bars in the aura revealing depression.

effective visionaries who tend to make their ideas become 'real' in three-dimensional terms, either on canvas or in other practical ways.

Some actors are of this type, though with greater evidence of the blues of the adept communicator. I have noticed in some of my workshops with actors that the very mystical mid-blue is often apparent — a great facility for actors who really wish to get 'inside' the author's mind or fully into character.

Other communicators like writers, teachers and those to whom language in its various forms generally is important tend to have a dominance of the relevant blue hues in the top half of the aura.

The healer

First and foremost, all healers, those who genuinely can assist others on their own healing quest, will always have significant patches of black. The black is essential and often manifests predominantly around the heart chakra, but it is also visible in the crown and, in all auras, in small patches around the base of the astral body.

Most of the psychic debris, as I call it, is found at the bottom of the auric field — like sediment, it is 'heavy' and sinks to the lower area of the emotional and mental body, waiting to be transmuted upwards by higher thinking and creative, unselfish actions. The psychic debris is the pain and the darkness we suffer in our lives as we grow, often with great difficulty, towards love and enlightenment.

The healer's aura always has one or two particular radiances to it. Of course, we are all healers and all play our part, but the healer of significance cannot be missed — they heal through their presence, irrespective of any other therapy they may use. A healer who can assist in bringing some physical easement to others through the radiation of energy will always display a vibrant, clear orange. It is quite distinctive and can often also be seen in the auras of those who have just been healed.

Healers whose thoughts are very effective, good prayer or intercessionary healers, will always have beautiful, clear violets and possibly amethyst as well as the mystical, mid-blues.

A good vibrant emerald and sometimes apple- or yellow-green, are also essential for someone engaged in the healing arts in some way or another. In the aura of a great friend of mine who was a healer while in this life, the green was clear and profuse around him at all times.

Rose is useful, but not essential in great volume in the aura of a healer, but especially loving souls on this path will show patches of silver and/or gold, especially those who are truly dedicated, with years of experience.

The healer's auric field is usually very expansive, having a soft, yet strong, feel to it. It is rather like being wrapped in a beautiful, supportive cushion enabling those who touch it to feel safe, secure and free. A true healer's aura is wonderful to behold.

Children and Auras

As children enter the world, their first years of life are devoted mainly to developing their energy bodies and physical selves. The development of the emotional body takes second place, temporarily. As they progress through the first six or seven years of their lives, the energy and physical bodies strengthen and then the emotional field seems to completely superimpose itself on the two lower levels.

The emotional form then starts to develop, climaxing in puberty between 12 and 14 years. The soft pinks, blues, clear reds and white-yellows are gradually replaced by the bright, sometimes volatile colours we more commonly associate with auras and especially the emotional body.

Many adolescents become aware of this change, not least through the deep and sometimes explosive emotional patterns they begin to experience. The process leads them to an awareness, at least subliminally, of their fast-developing 'colours' in line with their fast-unfolding emotional nature, and consequently they very often wear clothing that conceals or 'denies' this phenomenon. They may 'hide' their bright colours by choosing to wear dark browns, blacks and greys.

This period of emotional development is followed by an integration of the mental body, when we become mentally more aware, usually stabilising around 19 to 21 years. The fusing of the mental body with the physical, energistic and emotional levels of self should, at least in theory, lead to some kind of intellectual stability and maturity from where the individual is able and willing to think for him or her self without too much parental control or influence. This is the time when a child 'comes of age', a time for children to become our friends and equals, no longer the sweet young dependant infants we once knew, but adults, waiting to think and feel for themselves, flexing their own mental muscles and hearts in the challenging world into which they have been incarnated.

Adult life begins — the time in which to learn to manage our own personality, bringing its higher qualities to the fore, and giving our soul or higher self time to remind us that we are a spirit, a great and mysterious being, on the edge of a profound awakening and process of self-discovery, in which death and passing should be our glorious ascent into 'heaven', the higher realms of being.

The abstract mental self, the aspect of our nature we touch in deep meditation, the space from which clear ideas and thoughts come, is not part of this auric integration. It is more connected with the soul force, or higher self and thus links with the mental body via thought processes and the intuitive flow.

That which we call the aura is now in place, waiting for the time when the complete overshadowing of the spirit takes place and we glow with the glorious golden light of the soul.

Attuning to the Rays in your Own Aura

Exercise 9

1. Sit and relax somewhere quietly where you will not be disturbed for a while.

2. Use Exercise 4 to radiate and clear your aura and energy field.

3. Take three beautiful, energy-laden deep breaths, focusing your attention on the solar plexus (stomach area), feeling the power of your breath entering there as you inhale, and then spreading throughout your body as you exhale.

4. Give a special blessing to your angels and guides and thank them for the support and guidance they give to you.

5. Slowly, yet firmly, take your attention upwards into your head. Imagine as you do so that you are entering a large cinema with a magnificent blank screen in front of you, waiting to show the film.

6. The screen lights up with a beautiful picture of a great, old building, rather like a temple. Enjoy the image. The temple has a large, ornate door which slowly opens for you and you step inside.

7. Inside the building, the atmosphere is calm, tranquil and very welcoming.

8. Towards the front of this building you see a lone figure seated in the stillness. Radiating around the figure you can see a beautiful burst of light and many colours appear, surrounding the individual in a mantle of breathtaking glory and vibrant aura. There is a familiarity about this figure; as you move closer, it turns and smiles at you. It is you. The colours you can see are the rays and emanations of your own aura.

9. Enjoy this feeling for a few moments and observe what you see, remembering it all.

10. Eventually retrace your steps slowly through your temple until you are outside. The picture fades and you are now back in your room, sitting quietly, radiating beautiful light all around you.

Leave the exercise slowly, feet firmly on the floor, bring yourself gently back, opening your eyes slowly as you go.

Make a note of the colours you have seen and ask them to speak to you, remembering each ray has an angel who can help you understand what you have seen.

Make notes of anything you wish to keep for reference and say thank you for what you have learned.

Perceiving the Colours of Another's Auric Field
Exercise 10
An objective approach

1. Sit with your friend, some five or six feet between you. If they wish, they may stand up, but sitting is fine.
2. Ensure the light in the room is not too bright, although darkness is not necessary. A plain background may be useful in the early stages.
3. If you have not already done so, use Exercise 4 first to radiate your own light.
4. Inside you, there is a light-scanning device, in the centre of your head, sometimes called the third eye, an aspect of the pineal gland. It is your own radar. Consider your third eye for a few moments.
5. As directed by you, your third eye begins to scan and to view the radiations of light and colour around your friend. Eventually, with practice, patches and then swathes of colour will become apparent.
6. Relax and enjoy what you see.

At the end, ground yourself and radiate your light as usual, before awakening slowly to discuss with your friend what you have seen and what you have experienced. Let your imagination work and don't be timid, and notice the small things as well as the dramatic.

This is an objective approach, easier for some than others to achieve. As I have had such vision since I was a child, it comes easily to me, but I have had years of experience now, in Europe and the USA, teaching others to unfold their psychic and spiritual gifts sensibly and know that, with patience, one method or another will work to bring the subtle vision to the surface. The secret is simply to cultivate a relaxed, yet determined patience to succeed. And you will.

Don't be afraid to be creative with the exercises. The most important thing is to have high motivation to develop your awareness in order to become a more useful, aware and caring individual.

Always remember to use the radiation and clearing exercise before and after all others. With a little practice it will only take a minute or so and is vital.

A subjective approach

For some, equally effective is an 'inner' or subjective approach as opposed to the 'outer', objective method above.

1. Sit with a friend facing you.
2. Radiate and clear your energy.
3. Take your concentration inside your head and see the blank 'cinema' screen inside your forehead.
4. Bring to mind your friend and say their name inside your head.
5. Then imagine you can see their outline forming on your blank inner screen. Eventually, colours also appear, moving slowly around the form of your friend already in your picture.

6. Feel connected, yet not too close to your friend. Sense them and let the pictures develop inside your head.

Always trust your vision. It may be vague or indistinct initially, or even blank or non-existent. Eventually, with patient persistence, you will achieve a measure of success. The dynamic of believing and trusting what you perceive is very important; it will help you achieve many things. Banish doubts from your mind.

7. Conclude the exercise by clearing the pictures from your screen, then follow Exercise 4.

You can discuss your findings and experience with your friend. And, again, always say thank you to the angels and to the universe for the learning and growth you will experience.

CHAPTER 4
PSYCHIC CENTRES, CORDS AND KUNDALINI

To everything,
Turn! Turn! Turn!
There is a season,
Turn! Turn! Turn!
And a time to every purpose under Heaven ...
Ecclesiastes/Pete Seeger/The Byrds

I remember my reactions to the sight of the spinning wheels of light I saw as a child. Sometimes they emanated from people, sometimes from animals and flowers and often from the earth itself. I experienced a perplexing combination of wonder and awe, yet also a strange familiarity. I can recall seeing these incandescent vortices in my pre-birth dialogues with angelic entities; it is during this time that the chakras are programmed or 'geared' and then blended to form the perfect mix for our personality upon the earth. The gearing of these psychic centres, adopted by the individual for a lifetime, establishes the blend of forces he or she can absorb from the universe during that time, and thus the human nature he or she will reveal to the world.

Much has already been written about the chakras and a whole range of ideas and opinions exist as to their appearance, number and function. In this chapter, I offer some of the insights gained from my own vision of these centres of light. Everything here is based on my observations and subtle vision.

Energy and Chakras

As we move around our wondrous planet, we are affected by the subtle forces that flow across its surface. This provides a means by which we can cooperate and work in harmony with the earth and understand its nature as its qualities fluctuate from one place to another.

Because of our ignorance, we often build our roads and other infrastructure across these lines of force — ley lines (see Chapter 5) — with the consequence that when we drive across them, we may feel a sudden change or sensation — perhaps the hair stands up on the back of our necks or we may feel dizzy or light-headed for a moment. Occasionally, fear grips us as we develop an unjustified dislike of the place, or decide there is negative energy there. This is rarely, if ever, the case. As a race, we tend to fear what we do not understand, and try to change it rather than learn to adapt to it.

As the chakras visible in the subtle auras of people and animals connect with and absorb the radiations and forces from the universe, giving us power and helping us register information, they are in a constant state of flux and unfoldment, the apparent spinning and pulsing motion of their surface quickening and then slowing in a never-ending sequence of normal, healthy reactions.

As we enter each new situation, the interaction within the chakra system in our bodies modifies as some chakras become more prominent or active, and the role of others diminishes in response to the change. Whether we are simply physically crossing a ley line in a new location, or meeting someone for the first time, in a job interview, for example, if we remain confident, the chakras readjust and we treat the new situation as an adventure, a healthy part of our lives.

But if at these times, fear takes hold and we are unable to control our energy reaction (for example, through good breathing) and mental poise (through constructive, spiritually focused thoughts), our chakras can become fixed or blocked, we lose our adaptability, and so the key to healthy living is lost. Imbalance follows, with subsequent related mental and physical problems.

The Chakras or Psychic Centres

The chakra system looks like a series of brilliant, spinning disc-shaped lights, one above the other along the spinal column in the case of the larger spinal or major centres, with smaller points of light along lines radiating across the body for the smaller ones. Sometimes it can be likened to being covered with rows of beautiful fairy lights, the larger, more coloured ones spinning and radiating from the top of the head to the root of the spine.

The appearance of each chakra is essentially that of a spiralling wheel. Viewed from the front, they seem to have three layers or ridges converging at a central point that looks like a very small opening or 'window' (see Figure 7).

The spinning of the ridges, which all turn separately at different speeds, creates the impression of a spiralling vortex. Sometimes they spin very slowly, indicating an energy block and underabsorption, and can appear frozen or static in situations of shock or overexposure to difficult radiations and wave forms (for example, nuclear radiation, computers, mobile phones). This leaves the individual at risk to problems in the energy body unless remedied quickly by healing of some kind. (Bach Rescue Remedy is excellent for reinstating centre movement, especially in the solar plexus and the brow centres.) On the other hand, excessively fast spinning indicates overabsorption of energy.

Essentially, the spin of the chakras relates to each breath we take and alters with the changes in our breathing. However, these movements are extremely complex and any intellect-based analysis of chakras is usually very limited and inaccurate; they can only be understood through sound intuition.

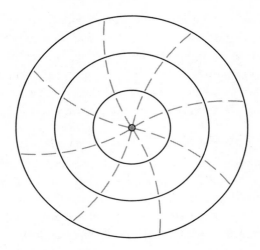

Figure 7   Front view of a chakra or psychic centre.

The profile of a chakra resembles a cone, rising out from the body and taking on a tube-like form that moves like an antenna within the aura of which it is a part (see Figure 8). It absorbs energy, which can be seen and sensed entering through the front of the centre; this is then assimilated into the whole system.

The chakras can be viewed psychically to exist at every level:

~   in the physical body as ductless or endocrine glands
~   in the etheric or energy body as clear spirals
~   in the astral or emotional body as bright, multicoloured discs, with firework-like bursts emanating from the edge
~   in the mental aura, also as spinning discs, but more floral in form, closer to the lotus of eastern tradition.

There are two main areas of consideration worthy of note here:

~   the relationship between the chakras and physical and mental health
~   their significance in understanding the destiny or life-pattern of the individual.

For a professional health worker or therapist, a knowledge or reasonable grasp of both ideas is essential. For everyone, these are probably the most significant issues we encounter in our lives. These psychic centres determine both our relationship with and access to the rest of the universe and the power it seeks to give to us via our own sun. They are the gateways to the spirit.

The Psychic Centres and Health

To be healthy or 'whole', it is necessary for us to absorb the full range of cosmic or divine force available to us. This force comes to us as a powerful divine pulse — indeed, our universe was created by one of these pulses in what we refer to as the Big Bang. As creatures with a variety of rhythms in us, we break down this pulse into a series of different sub-rhythms, or tones, and absorb them into the most appropriate areas and levels of our nature.

There are currently some thirteen centres visible to me as major centres (see Plate 8). Although this varies from person to person, us-ually nine or ten centres or chakras are found to be especially active in most people:

~ root
~ base
~ abdomen
~ solar plexus
~ heart
~ meta-heart
~ throat
~ mouth (sometimes)
~ brow
~ crown.

Each one can be viewed as a cog in our psychic mechanism. They are programmed together in a specific relationship before our birth, thus giving each of us our individuality. The centres

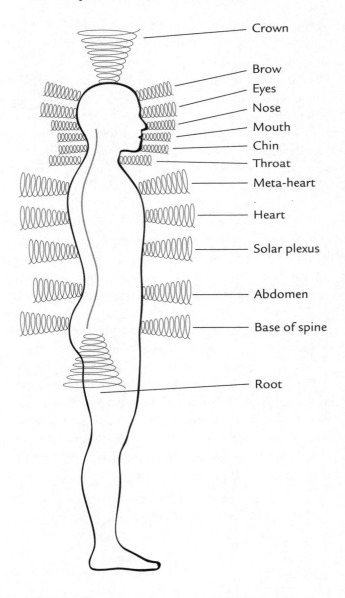

Crown

Brow
Eyes
Nose
Mouth
Chin
Throat
Meta-heart

Heart

Solar plexus

Abdomen

Base of spine

Root

Figure 8 Profile of the chakras or psychic centres.

are open, or clear, in order to allow a balanced blend of force to flow through us in our lifetime, enabling us to be the most effective individual of our type that we can be.

The problems, or blocks, occur when our emotional equilibrium is disrupted severely by shock or emotional dis-ease. Sometimes the blocks can occur because we are misusing our bodies and other diff-iculties emerge as we lose mental balance and flexibility and either become too rigid or fanatical in our thinking, or at the other extreme, too disparate, lacking focus and concentration.

Often, of course, our difficulties involve all three levels. The impact on us at one level ripples outwards and tends to affect everything else: mental problems produce unusual and difficult emotional responses; emotional trauma can impede effective mental input and management of experience and often produces etheric and then physical disruption and disease; emotional disruptions — fear, guilt, envy, hate — are the primary causes of most disease in our society and it is in the emotional chakras that much healing is often needed.

Our goal, for physical health, is a balanced life, with a varied pattern of activity designed to keep physical body, emotions and mind all exercised and developed adequately. Good diet and exercise; listening to inspiring music; viewing goodness and beauty around you; and engaging in creative activity and regular meditation and prayer will all continue to ensure a well-balanced life, along with the discovery of your purpose for this life:

> *Your work is to discover your work*
> *and then pursue it with all your heart.*
> Buddha

Clearing the psychic centres
Exercise 11
This exercise is another activity to be included in any spiritual diary or journal that you may keep. It has a truly wonderful effect on the psychic centres and opens them for improved absorption of cosmic and universal force. During this process, we are rediscovering how to breathe with the universe, increasing our health and vitality, opening the doors between the many levels of ourselves and integrating our physical, energistic, emotional, mental and soul planes, so that we may function more effectively.

I suggest this exercise is best done once or twice weekly as part of a regular meditation period. After a time, you will find that you can extend the exercise a little and become very conscious of the appearance of the centres and the colours revealed in them, and a real dialogue unfolds.

Keeping initially to the sequence outlined here will, in time, and with application and perseverance, help you achieve a great deal. Often more complex exercises are taught and these, in my experience, achieve no more. The psychic centres respond perfectly to the thoughts and energy involved in the simple mode of practice that follows.

1. Say a little prayer to the angel of the presence, the angel of your being, who seeks to assist you in the perfect management of your human nature, your light and your energies.
2. Clear and radiate your energies.
3. Continue to breathe rhythmically, remembering that, for your lifetime, you are in receipt of the most magnificent pulse of divine force and that you breathe in harmony with the cosmos.
4. Imagine the thirteen centres linked to your spinal column and, as you do, focus on the crown chakra. As you breathe in, direct your breath gently, yet firmly into and through

the crown chakra. As you exhale, imagine the force of your breath travelling down along the spine and out through the root centre underneath your spine, leaving a clear and open channel along the spinal column, from top to bottom. Do this for three consecutive rhythmic breaths and then allow your breathing to settle to its own gentle rhythm and flow.

5. Now, direct your attention to the root chakra. Once again, as you inhale, direct your breath and its energy, only this time upwards, from underneath your spine, flowing into and through the root chakra. As you exhale, the breath travels up the spinal channel and out through the crown chakra. Do this for three consecutive rhythmic breaths, before relaxing into your usual breathing.

6. Next, move your attention to the front of your body, level with the base of your spine. Again, use your 'imaging facility' to perceive the tube-like vortex of the base centre, running from in front of your spine, through your body and out the back. Direct the force of three more rhythmic breaths through the centre, seeing, feeling, the flow of breath as it travels in through the front of the centre as you inhale, and then out the back of your spine on exhalation. When you have done this, imagine a clear, open channel through this centre and then allow your breath to settle for a moment as you raise your concentration up to your abdomen.

7. Work through all the remaining centres: abdomen; solar plexus; heart; meta-heart; throat (Adam's apple); chin; mouth; nose; between the eyes; brow; and again through the crown. At the crown, imagine the energy travelling from top to bottom once more, being inhaled in through the crown chakra and exhaled through the root of the spine, leaving a clear and open channel.

8. Something beautiful happens here. You allow your breath to flow freely, and a magnificent column of light appears around the centre of the spine — a clear, transparent tube-like form. It pulses wonderfully and the turning motion of the astral and mental bodies or aura is adjusted perfectly as you enter a state of equilibrium. This enables much healing to take place. The hundreds of centres all over your psychic network also light up, producing pure, clear energy. Every cell in your body is glowing as you are wrapped in a great web linking hundreds of points of light.

9. Sound the words *I AM* slowly three times inside your head and then slowly step down through each centre along the spine, one at a time, pausing briefly at each one until you reach the root of the spine.

10. Then mentally direct each centre to adjust for everyday awareness and activity, or normal three-dimensional consciousness.

11. Imagine your aura, clear and radiating light. Feel your feet firmly on the floor or ground beneath you and gradually, connect with the earth. Make a few more rhythmic breaths before slowly opening your eyes. Sit or lie still for a few minutes before getting on with your everyday activities. And thank the angel of the presence for helping you.

Closing Down

It is worth mentioning here again that many people refer to 'closing down' the chakras or centres. I remember after one exercise on a course I was giving, a course member said to me, 'You forgot to close us down.' I gently joked that I didn't realise he was a shop or a redundant factory waiting to shut.

A teacher who believes he or she can close down the centres or chakras does not properly understand the mechanism or

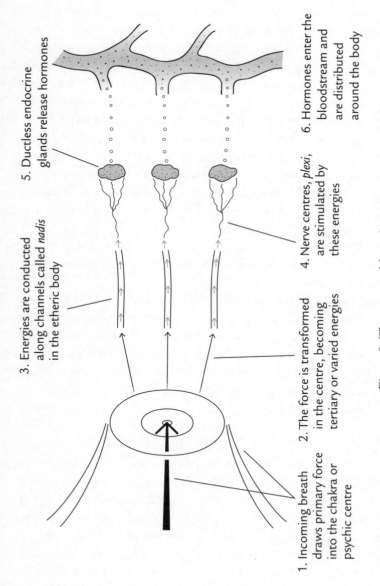

Figure 9 The process of force absorption.

5. Ductless endocrine glands release hormones

3. Energies are conducted along channels called *nadis* in the etheric body

6. Hormones enter the bloodstream and are distributed around the body

4. Nerve centres, *plexi*, are stimulated by these energies

2. The force is transformed in the centre, becoming tertiary or varied energies

1. Incoming breath draws primary force into the chakra or psychic centre

the nature of thought. We cannot 'close down'. What we have to do is allow ourselves to adjust to whatever activity we are engaged in at a given time. This we do naturally, all day long, unless we are shocked badly, or we experience some unusual psychotic pattern, usually induced through the brain.

If the exercises in this book are followed closely and patiently, and you are well-balanced mentally, no problems will be created; you can only benefit. If you have a history of mental or emotional problems, it is best to consult an experienced psychic and healer before embarking on a study such as this, or indeed anything involving intensive mental activity.

Please don't attempt to close your chakras or psychic centres; it is not possible — until you die and leave the planet altogether! It will only serve to confuse your subconscious.

Force Absorption

Each time we breathe, the process of force absorption takes place in our bodies (see Figure 9). It is useful to take a few moments to consider this process, to reflect on its function and to encourage it and give thanks for it and the health and healing it brings. Keep this idea in your mind to encourage daily renewal and physical, mental and emotional health.

Like many with psychic vision, I discovered that I could look into another individual's body and focus on a particular organ or physical mechanism. I can usually detect organ malfunction and pathological problems, and I can also observe the natural rhythms of the physical body and its relationship with the more subtle levels.

Observing the process of force absorption continually confirms for me the flow and interaction between ourselves and the cosmic energies of the universe.

Destiny, Purpose and the Psychic Centres

The psychic centres contain a vast wealth of information in their structures. With skill, psychic centre assessment can reveal much about the health and nature of an individual, so much more than even a whole battery of conventional psychometric testing and analysis. The centres cannot lie, though sound and experienced interpretation is crucial.

A little while ago, a new client came to me to have her aura and psychic centres viewed for a general interpretation and a little guidance. I did not know at the time that she was a university student 'investigating' people like me who claim to read auras and so on, to see how we use carefully loaded questioning to obtain the clues and answers we need from our unsuspecting clients.

I had looked at the rays in her aura, and the chakra relationship, before she had said anything besides 'Hello'. She was surprised, therefore, when I told her she had the perfect centre arrangement for someone who should study human nature and behaviour, and perhaps become a psychologist — I found out later that she was indeed reading psychology.

By looking at her chakras in the simple coded way that I have developed and refined over the years, I could see some of the potentials within her. I am usually able to gain a clear view of an individual and why they are here. Sometimes, what I say surprises the client but other times it confirms what they already knew and for which they sought confirmation. Often, I disagree with others' assessments, especially where it has been made using conventional models of evaluation. Of course, no one is infallible and some people are undoubtedly easier to read than others, but I find I am rarely very far off track in my assessment of potential and destiny. A young person once said to me, 'I don't know what I want from life' — the chakras will tell you what life wants from you!

The Technique of Psychic Centre Assessment

The following exercise in two stages will show you a simple approach to psychic centre assessment. When I view an individual for the first time I always see them as a mass of colours which I can then interpret as appropriate. You can easily learn to do the same.

Exercise 12 (Stage one)

First, ask a good friend to give you permission to make them the object of your research.

1. Go through the clearing and radiating exercise.
2. Relax and think of your friend.
3. Imagine they are either sitting or standing so you can see them clearly in your mind's eye or on the screen of your inner cinema.
4. Remember that your friend is a being of many levels, many layers of light. Give thanks for that and then ask your own angel of the presence to assist your focus in this exercise, to keep you in tune with the magic of what you behold.

The sign of the cross

As a youngster the phenomenon I began to perceive more and more clearly was the web of light as it interpenetrates the physical body — hundreds of points of light of differing sizes and intensities lit up the acupuncture points and the chakras.

At the Catholic Mass, individuals frequently make the sign of the cross, touching first their brow, their lips and then their hearts, completing the cross with a movement across from one shoulder to another. As they do this, a bright light always radiates on the forehead, or brow chakra, then in the middle of the chest as the heart expands. This is especially clear at Mass before the Gospel is read, where the sign of the cross on three major light centres — brow,

---

> mouth and heart — opens up the intellectual, creative and loving heart forces in the individual to the teachings.
>
> These chakras light up in perfect order and increase their rotational speed to improve the flows of the force through them, enabling a more integrated and profound relationship with the idea being shared. The whole individual, for a time at least, becomes more in tune, alive and receptive.
>
> During this phase of the Mass, to witness people glowing, their chakras pulsing like magical lights along the front and backs of their bodies, is a remarkable experience. If only they understood what they were doing — it could all mean so much more.

5. Next, imagine your friend in their great aura of light, full of vibrant, beautiful rays.

    Relax and enjoy the process of the vision forming — do not try to force it as that creates tension and produces the opposite of what we seek. Time, patience and persistence in these matters always brings reward.

6. Initially, you may see one or two colours, but eventually, a whole kaleidoscope will unfold before you. If you don't see the colours, you may feel them or sense what they are.

7. Go through the clearing and radiating exercise briefly. Always remember — be patient, trust what you see and do not allow doubts to impinge on your mind. You must learn to trust. And be bold — it is a natural ability in you that we seek to unfold.

When you have mastered Stage one, your next task is to familiarise yourself a little more with the meanings of the colours outlined in the previous chapter. It is not necessary to learn them off by heart. Just become acquainted with them — but not simply intellectually; develop a feel for them, encouraging a dialogue between them, their angels and you. All the processes in this book involve first the intuition, then the creative, higher psychic mechanism and thirdly, the intellect. Therefore a primarily intellectual approach will constrict your efforts.

The Order of the Psychic Centres

Now to understand the colour coding or colour priority system that the subconscious will show to us. With all exercises involving levels of awareness beyond three dimensions, any interpretation or method of analysis is based on compromise because it happens in the left side of the brain. It is even possible for apparently opposing ideas, contradictory descriptions of a psychic principle, both to be correct. There are many reasons for these discrepancies, the degree of mental and spiritual unfoldment of the observer being the prime factor. However, it is also because, in the higher, multidimensional layers of our existence, while there are core truths, there are a great number of ways that they can be expressed.

The value of the exercise that follows was most powerfully demonstrated to me when I observed an exceptionally gifted clairvoyant observing and interpreting the chakra sequences of some students on a course in the early 1980s. This experience 'set me on fire': it has enthralled and stimulated me ever since, and was largely responsible for the path I have followed in my work.

Exercise 12 (Stage two)

Use a pad and coloured pencils for this exercise. Seek the permission of one or two friends or family to act as subjects for your research. You may find it more productive to practise the technique in their presence, face to face, rather than at a distance but, with experience, you will find either way effective.

1. Go through the clearing and radiating exercise briefly.
2. Relax and focus on the person you are working with.

3. Ask for their colours — request that their current colour sequence be shown to you. This may appear either super-imposed over their physical body; slightly to one side of them; through your inner vision, inside your head, in your inner viewing chamber; or they may appear like a set of traf-fic lights. All approaches are equally valid and effective, and again, it is simply a matter of practice, persistence and trust. You are seeking the colour sequence and attuning to it.

4. As the first colour is given to you, draw a coloured circle on your paper, adding others beneath it, as they are revealed. Initially, you may be shown one or two colours, but in time, you will be able to view seven, eight or more in sequence.

    If you feel your inner vision is still limited and you don't see the colours, then feel them. This is easily done by link-ing your heart centre with your head (brow) centre and crown centre. Simply imagine that all three psychic centres, first the heart, then the brow and finally the crown, are joined for the purpose of this exercise. They are linked by a cord of clear light. As these three centres work together, you may begin to sense the colours as easily as some can see them — feel and trust what is there.

5. Once you have your list of colours, we can match them symbolically to the psychic centres. The colour emanations and combinations from the centres vary from individual to individual and from time to time. Ultimately, all psychic centres will radiate all colours, blending as they spin, first to produce a white centre, then gold–white, which signifies the presence of a perfect soul; and only a perfect human being can reveal such a soul.

The simplest symbolic matching is as follows:

a. Reds, crimsons and aubergines — root and base centres
b. Oranges — abdominal centre
c. Yellows (not gold) — solar plexus centre
d. Greens — heart centre
e. Turquoise — meta-heart centre
f. Mid-blues — throat/neck/mouth centres
g. Violet/purples — brow and eye centres
h. White — crown centre
i. Rose — heart centre

Silver can relate specifically to the heart centre, but with different indications and meaning to either rose or green.

Gold usually indicates a crown centre connection but is applicable to all other centres, especially the heart.

6. Ask each colour you have recorded to talk to you, to unfold its higher meaning for you. Listen, see and feel what you are told and make note.

7. When you have heard and seen everything you can — experience will make this clear to you — then briefly go through the clearing and radiating exercise and return to see what you have noted.

8. Discuss this with your friend and notice how, while talking and sharing, you will gain and express fresh insights about the colours and what they are saying. This is a particularly dynamic and important part of the exercise and is eventually the most revealing and interesting. Talk, see and feel.

With practice, the colours and their sequence will become easily and quickly visible. The discussion and interpretation then takes longer and becomes most important. Some people are easier to attune to and read than others. Usually, the more psychically awakened the individual, the more open and accessible they are from a psychic point of view.

In an assessment, the psychic mechanism in you will help you perceive the chakra colour sequence you are seeking to observe — you use mainly your own solar plexus, brow and eye centres or neck and throat centres and your heart centre. Again, this will vary from individual to individual as we are all made differently and at different stages in our unfoldment.

Some Methods of Chakra Analysis or Assessment

In the sample sequences that follow, you will see how to start to interpret the patterns that show themselves in chakra assessment. These can indicate the emergence of a particular period or cycle in a person's life; or, in type analysis, the tendency towards certain types of behaviour.

Sequence A

Green — *heart centre*
Blue — *throat*
Yellow — *solar plexus centre*

Cycle analysis

For me, one of the most interesting aspects of an assessment of the psychic centres is the manner in which it reveals rhythms or cycles of change in a person's life.

For example, where the heart chakra is revealed first (symbolised by greens), a simple cycle analysis can be made as follows.

The current phase will be a time of balancing for the individual. The domination of the green/heart chakra will almost certainly herald a period of outer change and growth preceding the desired equilibrium and harmony. It is what I refer to as an 'itchy feet' period, a time where we wish to change things in us and around us.

With practice, you will become increasingly able to see and sense these rhythms and cycles and know how intense they are likely to be. Not all change periods bring dramatic change; generally the deeper and richer the green, the more profound the changes will be. You will also learn how to sense the nature of the cycle, its intensity and its likely duration.

In Sequence A, the blue of the throat and yellow of the solar plexus follow the green of the heart.

If you ask which is the next colour to influence or govern, you may be told it is yellow.

Where the yellow/solar plexus governs the next phase, you find the practical, mental aspect of the ray will rule the cycle. This means a period to attend to detail, implement plans and generally deal with the logical aspects of life. Implementation is usually what is required. I often find that the yellow/solar plexus ray is dominant, or will be dominant, around the time of an examination or assessment of some practical significance. Also, it is usually the ray of perseverance and means hard, but rewarding work ahead.

As well as its link with the intellect or the logical mind, the solar plexus also has links with the astral or emotional body. If the yellow indicated by the solar plexus is very dark or brown-edged, we are then seeing an intellectual period impeded by ambitious tendencies or ruthlessness.

However, if the yellow seems to have pale or whitish patches in it, this will reveal lack of confidence and anxiety.

In Sequence A, if the blue of the throat is revealed as the second ray, rather than yellow, we can expect the individual to go into a calmer, possibly more contemplative period, though this may often be a period of ideas (especially if the blues are pale or sky blues). The darker or mid-blues can reveal a deeper, sometimes mystical period requiring much prayer and reflection, even a retreat period, a time for personal space. The lighter blues will encourage a time for communication or negotiation.

Sequence B

Blue — *throat centre*
Yellow — *solar plexus centre*
Green — *heart centre*

The sequence that follows is that of the young psychology student I referred to earlier, when she came to see me for the first time (she subsequently returned to interview me further in relation to her thesis). I made both type and cycle analyses of what was revealed to me.

Type analysis
The combination of blue and yellow was most telling. The intense blue of the throat revealed a very engaging, communicative individual who could connect well with others. She was able to easily draw out from others the deeper issues in their minds and people would sense that this was someone who would listen to what they said. This quality is ideal for those working in a caring, supportive role and needing insight into human nature; essential also for psychologists, counsellors and therapists dealing with human mental and emotional issues. Such souls can listen to and understand 'stories' of all kinds.

The vibrant, accompanying yellow was equally revealing and interesting. It would understand and interpret what the blue was hearing, and this indicated a clear capacity to assess what was being said in a structured and intelligent manner, and to make interesting deductions.

The presence of the heart ray, green, meant that this person had a balancing or healing potential within her, so necessary in any work with people. The intensity of the green also illustrated a reasonable capacity for breadth of thinking, as well as logical patterns in her mind (the blue also does this to some degree). Most importantly though, the green/heart ray provides a capacity for empathy, compassion, yet also detachment.

Cycle analysis

The cycle assessment showed firstly that the subject seemed to be in a period useful for research and open creative thinking lasting for several months (throat/blues).

The relative position of the yellow/solar plexus ray indicated a period of structure and ordering the ideas that the blue had fed through. The student was to face examinations during this time and was also planning her thesis which included the collation of information.

When I saw her some six months later, the colour/chakra order had changed to:

Green
Yellow
Blue

The green/heart ray was now in dominance and heralding a per-iod of change and exploring new territory — ideal for experimentation and taking risks and facing new experiences.

The Cycles of Life

Once you have the chakra order, it is really a question of practice to establish how you see, feel and read the cycles that are waiting in someone's life and how you offer your client guidance. Remember that inevitably the flow of life will carry them on the path it has set for them, but that they will have choices to make about how they treat the information you provide.

It is not the psychic or visionary's role to control another's life patterns and limit their thinking about the possibilities before them. It is more an exercise in encouraging the creative endeavours of the individual, offering advice and support to help them understand the complex patterns in which we all live and grow. It is quite remarkable, and indicative of a higher

---

Reflection

At this point, it is good to pause for a while to reflect and consider the cycles of life.

Think of the seasons for a while, the contrasts between the extremes, summer and winter, autumn and spring, and how all are important components of an unfailing rhythm, ushering welcome changes in pace and purpose into our lives.

Consider how night and day, sunset and dawn, all provide their own essential magical quality and temper our experience perfectly. Quickening, then slowing, pausing, then growing. Wakening and sleeping.

We need our rhythms, our cycles, our contrasts.

The more sensitive we become to cycles, the more we can understand them and cooperate with them.

Look back on your life and see what cycles you can find.

---

intelligence at work, how the perfect chakra and energy sequences always seem to emerge to enable us to progress through the next phase of our lives and the experiences it will bring.

After much practice, you will begin to see larger patterns in your clients' lives that are not purely for a few months, but anything up to seven years or more in duration.

Birthdays and anniversaries

Sometimes it may be difficult to establish the colour sequence. The colours may seem to bubble around or be moving, changing positions. The most common reason for this is that they are being viewed either on or close to a birthday or other very significant anniversary. Major change or shifts in our life patterns often occur close to a point of personal astrological significance, sometimes our own birthday or that of someone close to us, or the anniversary of the passing of a loved one, which is, after all, another birth.

I need to move!

Violet   —   head centre
Green   —   heart centre
Yellow   —   solar plexus centre
Rose   —   heart centre

This client had had a difficult period, almost depressive, where she experienced a great deal of negative thinking, many doubts about her future, especially her need to sell her house so that she and her husband could move to another home closer to his new job.

The violet/head centre vibration had stimulated her imagination but, as we often do, she expected and imagined the worst. It is not the violet that makes this happen, merely a human tendency. In fact the presence of violet generally gives us the opportunity to become more 'inner-directed' in our living and to pause and use our imagination creatively to change our reality and experience.

This lady had taken the alternative option and was a little depressed. The green/heart ray suggested changes on the horizon — including the sale of her house. With her negative thoughts in mind, though, she told me that there were several houses like hers for sale in the same street, some in better positions than hers and also we were in an economic recession at the time. I pointed out that if it was the right time for her to move, then move she would. Profound change and a house move were indicated soon. A day or so after our meeting, the green/heart centre began to dominate (the change coincided with her mother's birthday) as I had observed it would and a few days later she received an offer for her house which resulted in a sale and the move she had wanted took place.

When this happens, by encouraging the person you are viewing to relax a little, you will usually manage to stabilise things and the sequence will become clearer to see.

Some Typical, General Colour Meanings for Cycle Analysis

Green — heart
A period of change and growth. Often connected with financial change, house move, job change and so on. Intensity varies. Often heralds a busy spell. Can be frustrating in the middle of the cycle. With young people, the birth of a child. In men, job change and the birth of a child often come close together.

Blue — throat
Usually a time for lateral thinking, creativity and ideas. If the colour is very dark, the individual can be a little overwhelmed by the volume and intensity of the thoughts. Mid-blues suggest a period for mental space and easier pace of living. Light blue breeds optimism and it can also be a good time for communication and clarity.

Yellow — solar plexus
Usually indicates a practical time. A 'nitty-gritty' phase for dealing with the implementation of ideas. A time for analysis and action. Good for 'straight down the line', focused thinking. If orange creeps in, a need to open up to broader, less emotional influences is indicated.

Violet — head
A time for inner growth and reflection, creative use of the imagination and for spiritual activity and artistic endeavour. Not always an especially practical phase, often leading to depressive feelings and oversensitivity when tired — a time when more sleep and rest is needed.

Purple — head
When a purple hue is visible may be a time of vivid dreams and powerful psychic experience and heightened sensitivity.

Always a time for patience. A true 'purple patch' is when we are confident and have constructive, forward-looking visions — a great gestation period.

Silver — heart and head

Always denotes a very intuitive period. Rarely seen as the top colour, more an influence on other colours.

Gold — crown and heart

Again, rarely seen as the top colour but, if visible, shows a very special opportunity to connect with the inner realm and spiritual wisdom. Generally heralds a period of calm.

Rose — heart

Usually high when family and relationship issues are or will be under scrutiny. Often indicative of romantic possibilities, or powerful family issues to the fore. The rose ray can contain indications of possible conception and pregnancy in women.

Orange — abdomen

Orange very rarely seen as top colour. When in top three or four colours, usually health or energy issues are important; can be indicative of a need for healing or that therapy is being received. Sometimes, if the orange is extremely heavy and almost sticky, toffee-like in appearance, it can denote a sexual or even promiscuity problem.

Red — root

Red very rarely seen as top colour. Most undesirable when visible in top three or four chakras. Indicative of a period of frustration and excessive need or use of personal will. This can indicate exhaustion or excessive stress, especially where the red/root centre is higher than orange/abdomen. This shows that more vitality is being used by the individual than is being absorbed and, if it persists over many weeks, will lead to exhaustion, collapse and breakdown, both physical and possibly emotional.

Destiny

A chakra or psychic centre assessment also reveals to us one other very important aspect of any individual's life pattern — destiny. The destiny of an individual derives from the commitment we make before our life on earth begins; it is the guiding purpose behind each incarnation.

Generally, our destiny involves everyday things and people. We draw to ourselves those whose experiences we need to help us to grow and unfold our true nature and power. The 'magnetism' of our soul, or solar self, knows our destiny and governs our aura and chakra radiations. But we can often find our way more dynamically (not necessarily easily) through life when we identify an attraction to work that not only serves our selves, but also benefits humanity. The idea of a calling or vocation is not always grand in nature, but is always important and ultimately defining.

A good chakra reader can glimpse the destiny of a client and assess the nature of the working life that will most likely lead the client in the direction of that destiny. Sometimes, however, it may be possible, or desirable, only to indicate broadly where the person might go next, using generalisations such as 'working with people' or 'being in communications or media' or 'teaching or instructing others' and so on. Usually there are many doors to go through on the way, taking one step at a time. At other times, though, it is quite clear that the client should abandon all other things as soon as possible in favour of their true path, and the assessor can be quite specific as to what is required in order for them to fulfil their purpose here.

The sensitivity of the reader will help to know what is best shared. And rarely does such information 'go against' the deeper feelings of the client — we always know in our hearts what we have to do, even though we may sometimes be inclined not to listen or believe what we see or hear.

The heart map

Though there is a sequence that you can follow using the whole major chakra system to connect with one's unfolding destiny, the heart is good place to start.

Exercise 13

1. Relax. Use the clearing and radiating exercise. Thank the angel of the presence for being with you.
2. Be aware of the column of light along your spinal column, with the major chakras rotating brilliantly along the length of the spine, from root to crown.
3. Imagine the root centre, active and powerful, a beautiful cone of light extending outwards from the root of the spine. Remember that this links you with the earth and the purpose behind your present incarnation.
4. Next, imagine the beautiful, glorious heart centre, a cone of magical force turning and radiating green, silver, purple and golden light. In the heart, the purpose of your life is understood — here we find the map of your life, your destiny.
5. The light from the root centre then travels gently up the spinal column until it reaches the heart. As it touches the heart, it fuses with the heart-light, a glorious rising sun at dawn.
6. As this light expands, it speaks to you. It reveals to you your destiny, your pathway. Allow the picture to form.

   (If you are guiding someone else through this visualisation, look into the heart as the energies fuse, and be aware of any constructive, helpful images that come to you that will help your subject.)

7. When you have seen your heart map, heard your inner voice or felt an understanding, go through Exercise 4 briefly before returning to make any notes you wish.

You may be fortunate and glimpse the heart map quite soon, but usually images come slowly and gradually as we become increasingly ready and able to deal with them. This will vary from person to person, but your soul will know what is best for you. It may take several or indeed many attempts at this exercise before your heart shows you clearly what you wish to see. But remember, persistence and patience are the keys. All things come to those who wait.

Self-development Exercises

There are many self-development exercises that can be worked effectively through the chakra system. Here are a few more of those I use most often with clients and in workshops.

Dissipating anger
Exercise 14

1. Clear and radiate your energies and then ask your angel of the presence for assistance.
2. See the energy of the base chakra. It is deep red, strong and powerful.
3. Visualise also the heart chakra, this time predominantly vibrant apple green in colour. The heart as always is full of love, abundant with wise forces.
4. Next, gently allow the deep reds of the base chakra to rise slowly upwards along the spinal column. As they do so, the forces of will and strength, where the seeds of anger and aggression take hold, rise upwards, the deep reds gradually transmuting into a wonderful rose-pink light. As it enters the heart and pours through its centre, it forms a perfect rose flower, fringed with emerald green.

5.   Enjoy the flowering in the heart as it manages the forces of will and transmutes them into love and good will. Feel it and see it. It is a beautiful experience.
6.   Give thanks for the transmutation that has taken place within you and for the help you have been given.
7.   Radiate and clear your energies and then return to normal consciousness.
8.   Plan and then follow through with an unsolicited act of kindness for another, particularly for someone you feel you do not especially like or with whom you have been in conflict in some way. Its effect will be all the more powerful.

Practised often, this is a very liberating exercise.

Connecting with your intuitive flow

The intuitive flow is the whole intuitive process and works through the integrated activity of the chakras of the crown, the heart, the brow and the eyes.

Intuition is the true inner voice, the voice of the soul. It is active in all soul-searching or spiritual activity, but in fact seeks to help us in *all* situations so that we can live our life as effectively as possible and pursue our true path; we need only allow ourselves to properly cultivate our contact with it and listen to what it can tell us.

Though the intuition is a subject worthy of a book in itself and too great to consider in more detail here, it would be wrong, in any consideration of the psychic centres, not to make mention of it.

With this exercise, which was taught to me by my inner guidance, Heartstar, you can practise feeling your intuition flow and enjoy the inspiration it brings.

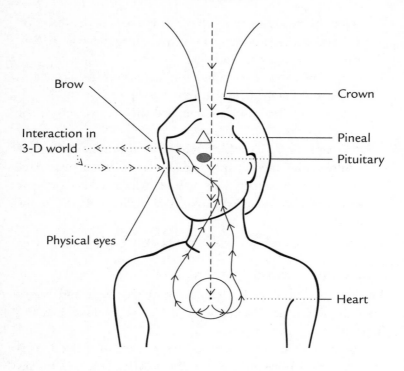

Figure 10 The intuitive flow.

Exercise 15

1. Clear and radiate your energies. Welcome your angelic support and help — it is always there.
2. See your chakras in all their magnificence, especially those major centres linking with your spine and glandular system.
3. Be especially aware of the light pouring in through the crown of your head, where the great divine flow appears to enter your being (see Figure 10). It is full of wonderful forces, ideas and inspirations; it is unlimited and is the beginning of the intuitive flow. It knows that in truth, you can do and be anything you choose.

4. As this light travels past the pineal gland, you will see pictures, images, have many ideas and inspirations — anything creative and uplifting like this is the spirit coming in: an in-spiration.
5. Allow and encourage this light and these inspirations to flow down to your heart. There you can feel them and let them gestate for a few moments.

    Remember, your heart is the seat of your life map; it knows your destiny and its wisdom will flow back up into your head — perfect intuition, knowledge from within.
6. This flow is then drawn upwards by the magnetic pull of the pituitary gland and the brow chakra and, as it returns to your head, the ideas are filtered to allow only the most useful and accessible ones to come into your mind. The heart is the centre of discrimination and understanding and it will have done its job for you.
7. Once you have your idea, your vision, then pursue it. The heart may well surprise you in its choice, but follow it into action. Visualise the idea as if it has already taken place and take what practical steps you can to bring about its manifestation. Be patient and trust your intuition.
8. Finally, the intuitive flow reaches your eyes, which respond to the three-dimensional world as you work towards the completion of your goal or idea. Your physical eyes report the effects of your actions.

At each stage in the progress towards your goal, use the intuitive flow to further unfold your inspiration.

Hand-sensing the Major Chakras

This is a useful exercise for those who are working in some form of therapeutics, though it should not really be used as a diagnostic technique. It is essential that good clairvoyant vision and sentience are used in combination to avoid errors; certain techniques, such as protection techniques, which are widely taught, can restrict the auric field and chakra system and limit the energy flow and can thus limit the effectiveness of the process.

Exercise 16

A partner is needed for this exercise.

1. Seat your partner on a comfortable upright chair or stool, preferably without a solid back to it. Facing them, sit a few feet away.
2. Go through Exercise 4 together, clearing and radiating energy.
3. Next, make contact with your partner's aura very gently, by stepping slowly into their aura space and standing behind them, resting your hands on their etheric body a couple of inches above their shoulders, with the palms of your hands facing downwards (see Figure 11).

    You will easily find the edge of the etheric field as you will feel a gentle resistance. Your hands will gently bounce off their shoulders, just like touching an inflated balloon. With practice and patience you may also find the nerve centres in the palms of your hands, fingertips and thumbs will give you a sensation, anything from a slight dull ache, to a tingling or warmth. This energy awareness will grow as you practise and can be experienced equally in the etheric bodies of other living entities — animals, plants, trees and so on.
4. Move to the side of your partner placing one hand in front of them, the other behind, both in line with the brow of the head.

    Again, you wish to sense the etheric body, so initially have the palms of your hands some distance away from their physical body. Slowly and gently bring the hands inwards towards the physical and etheric bodies until you feel the slight bounce again. The distance from the physical body at which you sense or feel the chakra will vary from person to person, from chakra to chakra.

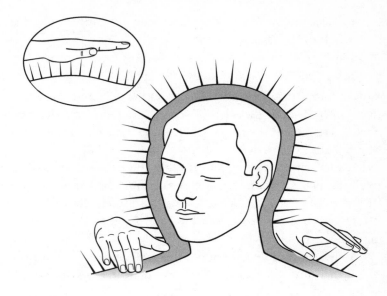

Figure 11 Hands resting above the shoulders, on the etheric body.

5. After a few moments, gently move your hands outwards again, away from the body until all sensation has stopped in your hands. Then shake your hands from the wrists very gently for a few seconds.

6. Repeat this gentle process along the spinal column, sensing all the major chakras.

    Remember to be gentle and careful. It is a privilege to be allowed to experience another being at such an intimate level, so as always be sensitive and respectful.

7. Using both hands, bring the activity to an end by first sensing the root chakra, underneath the spine, and then sense the energies moving through the crown chakra.

    This can be done most effectively by bringing your hands together slowly, one on either side of each chakra as it radiates upwards and downwards respectively into the spinal column. You will sense a slight resistance across the width of the chakra vortex.

8. Finally, give thanks and then move away from your partner, using Exercise 4 again briefly.

I have found that you can stand on either side and use either hand in front or at the back of your partner. Just do what you feel is natural and comfortable. However, you may notice that the sensations experienced in each hand are different. This is due to polarity, and one hand (usually the left, but not always) will possibly feel warmer and generally heavier than the other. It is the energy circuit in each of us that creates this sensation, energy tending to move from the right hand to the left more noticeably.

As always, make a note of your experiences in your spiritual journal. You are seeking to learn, so treat everything with respect and a sense of awe. In this way, all activities of the kind described in this book, where you are perceiving the subtle layers of being, will never become routine. They will always be fresh and exciting.

Kundalini

Essentially, the Kundalini or serpent energy is the superelectric charge in us that fires up and down our spinal column. We are aware of this energy most of all at times that are exciting and emotionally charged. This is why, when we go to a football match, for example, we feel compelled to stand, shout and even sing as we get more and more excited as the Kundalini is fired within us.

Ecstasy of all kinds is a manifestation of this energy as it races up and down the spine, often arching our backs as it does so, hitting us in the head, sometimes with great force. We can experience this in powerful, spiritual ecstasy, in sexual orgasm and other moments of great excitement.

When seen, it moves through the spinal chakra network and, sometimes called 'serpent fire', looks like a great charge of electricity that flashes up from a point near to the base of the spine, zig-zagging and spiralling around the chakras. Symbolically, control of this force is celebrated by the Rod of Caduceus, the symbol of Hermes Trismegistus, the Sword of St Michael slaying the dragon/serpent and in many other images. Controlling this power is pivotal in mastering ourselves and the forces within us. When this is achieved, the 'light in our heads' truly shines and we become 'full of light', enlightened and spiritually awakened.

The pattern of movement has three phases and appears like two serpents coiling back and forth over each other, circling each chakra in turn. When out of control, many different effects on our health can be identified — asthma, migraine, eczema and other allergic reactions, epilepsy and fitting, vertigo, for example. This happens because the 'brakes' are not applied to the two vertical Kundalinis by the third Kundalini that enters the system close to the solar plexus.

Many claim to have 'Kundalini experiences', which are most often manifestations of a temporary adjustment in this 'inner lightning' rather than enlightenment.

A Catholic priest came to see me from Ireland because he was having some unusual psychic experience. As always, it was easy to see the adjustment in his Kundalini that was taking place at that time. He is genuinely a man of prayer, a real celibate, who has astounding forces unfolding within him. This adjustment was not induced by unwisely performing Kundalini exercises *(I strongly advise the reader against attempting **any** such exercise)*, but this was simply a natural phase of his unfoldment with whose management he needed help.

As a general rule, if you suspect you have a similar problem, go back to Exercise 11, which is the best thing to use in most circumstances. However, serious problems should receive expert help, either from a good clairvoyant of some experience and reputation who also understands energies and healing forces, or a very experienced teacher of yoga.

Dance and rhythm are interesting examples of the effects of Kundalini movement. Dance can offer a controlled and structured pattern for the heightening of awareness and is therefore often used in magical and spiritual practice, and a rocking feeling is often felt by healers when tuning into the energy of their patients.

Musical rhythms get our feet tapping and urge us to dance, and young children, whose Kundalini forces are more volatile and unpredictable than those of adults, are especially prone to involuntary dancing and jigging. Next time you see some children running around and playing, imagine the powerful movement of the serpent fire in them as they hop, skip and jump.

I smile when I think of how my own daughter, who is a musician, would try to stand still while on the phone to a boyfriend, but would nonetheless keep hopping from one foot to the other unable to resist the Kundalini as it snaked up and down her back, rocking from side to side as it moved!

Cords and Emotional Ties

Much has been said about the psychic cords we create between ourselves and others. I can recall many strong images from my childhood of tubes of coloured light that seemed to radiate from one person to another, primarily from the solar plexus, but also from the abdomen and the heart.

These psychic cords are evident at moments of great emotional surge and are about our relationships with each other and the links we form. The strength and dynamic of the cord varies from connection to connection and with the intensity of the link. When we fall in love, the cording from the heart will dominate much of the time, giving as much energy as it takes as the cord is really a 'thought tube' that links two people so they can share their lives, thoughts and feelings.

The cords are rather like umbilical cords, and it is interesting how a mother, after the birth of her child, can take some time to adjust to the child and its energy being detached from her own, linked only by an invisible cord once the physical one has been broken and the child is beginning its own life. The mother and child and other members of the family will usually develop strong emotional links and cordings. Many of these will be through the heart, but also through the solar plexus, and some in the abdomen.

Solar plexus cords are often extremely emotionally charged and may seem to tug on us at times. How often, just before the telephone rings, do we feel a pulling sensation in our solar plexus, only to discover someone we are emotionally close to is calling and may need a listening ear or a helping hand.

The cords to the abdomen are often the most manipulative. It is from the abdomen that we frequently seek to control and manipulate others, sometimes even using material and sexual power to do it. This will always lead to disaster and much pain for those concerned, especially if linked to a strong emotional cording in the solar plexus trading in fear. Phoney political and spiritual leaders often use this approach. Such manipulative people will accompany their actions with such words as 'if you loved me, ... '; there is always an element of emotional blackmail. Sadly, people skilled at using such cordings effectively often do not realise what they do and are usually able to see it in others, rather than in themselves. These great manipulators are often highly critical of others, but do not take criticism well, however constructive it may be.

Once we have linked sexually, through intercourse, we form incredibly powerful cords. They are very strong and remain so for most of our lives. Promiscuity, therefore, can be disastrous, as it results in numerous cords being formed with many sexual partners. Where the heart cording is weak or absent in our relationships, this can create enormous problems for ourselves, if not immediately, then later in life. This weakens us considerably and makes it extremely difficult for us to form long-term, deeply loving relationships. It is more difficult for women than men when this happens; they are much more vulnerable at this level because they are slightly more energy responsive and are more open to negative effects than men. Highly sexed individuals are nearly always manipulative, and promiscuous people are usually condemning themselves to a painful, lonely life. Promiscuity is often caused by poor heart cording with one or both parents earlier in life.

Release from cording

The remedy is actually fairly simple, if not easy. We have to learn two things. Firstly, it is very important to build our relationships through our hearts and not our fears and our need for sex and power. Secondly, we must learn detachment. This is best done through regular practice of the clearing and radiating exercise and regular meditational exercises (see Appendix). Regular meditation strengthens the heart, opens the intuitive flow and helps us to feel, without being overwhelmed — compassion and empathy rather than sentimentalism and sympathy.

We should practise love in our lives, seeking to:

~ be givers, rather than takers
~ help others be free and joyful, rather than being in our lives for us to lean on
~ enable others, rather than seek to control them
~ live in the present, not allowing our cords to drive our energy and vitality into the past, hooking on to old ideas, past experiences and redundant feelings.
~ forgive.

The practice of forgiveness is particularly important.

There are many techniques, some of which I have explained in my book Being Loving is Being Healthy. There are many ways of releasing, letting go and forgiving. In extreme cases, we should perhaps seek professional guidance and spiritual counselling so that we can really let go of the past and live fully in this moment.

Exercise 17

1. Think of the person or the situation you can identify as being a focus of resentment, of emotional tension, hate, fear or simply sorrow.
2. Imagine them to be a beautiful butterfly, sitting in the palm of your hands.
3. Bless them and wish them to be free to enjoy the glory of life and their destiny. Wish them well.
4. Then lift your upturned hand up towards your mouth and gently blow them away, seeing them fly high, flapping their wonderful wings as they soar upwards and free, off into life. Well done.

Now they are free, and so are you. Practise this often; the more freedom you give, the more free you become. This is love in operation.

CHAPTER 5
THE LIGHT OF THE WORLD

Places we love exist only through us,
Space destroyed is only illusion in the constancy of time
Places we love we can never leave,
Places we love together ...

... When you go, space closes over like water behind you,
Do not look back: there is nothing outside you,
Space is only time visible in a different way,
Places we love we can never leave.

Ivan V. Lalic

I was standing in the centre of Frankfurt-am-Main in Germany, waiting to catch a tram. It was a crisp, early, spring morning and I was due to see some clients and also to sign a few copies of my books in an inner-city bookstore.

My attention was suddenly drawn upwards, to look at the many tall buildings and the light I could see around them, as they nestled around the river Main on its powerful flow through the centre of this bustling city. It was quite a remarkable sight, the bands of bright yellow and blue energy, wrapped around Frankfurt, radiating and pulsing as the city buzzed with its daily activities.

This wonderful rainbow of light reminded me once again that life, and everything in it, has many dimensions. Cities, communities, nations, planets — they are all entities, organic and alive, growing and developing through spiritual, mental and emotional patterns of their own. Frankfurt was revealing its particular vibration to me and affording a special insight into its nature and being.

Its light and energy, its aura, showed a dominant, clear, hard-edged, deep-yellow ray, useful in a financial community, where so much logical and practical thinking is required. But such a resonance can breed obsessive patterns of behaviour among those caught up in its light, where logic and the acquisition of money and material wealth rule. Individuals can easily feel dwarfed, intimidated, marginalised and unloved in such an environment, making existence there a little brutal. There is often a higher-than-usual turnover of staff and also a distinct lack of the connection that helps us feel we belong.

However, dribbling into the yellow ray was a shimmering blue band of creative power; an intense light that brings with it honour and truth and a more reflective, inspiring and less clinical mood. This will promote a more flexible approach and enable creative solutions to be found to seemingly intractable problems that arise, and it will tend to inspire some of those working within its influence (especially those open, adaptable individuals) to strive for higher, longer-term ideals, rather then short-term personal gain.

This is not to imply that Frankfurt is an especially hostile city in need of redemption. Indeed, I have a great affection for it and its people are kind and helpful. But its energy field, as revealed through its aura, is a complex blend, not only of the light and energy of its people, but also its vegetation, buildings, institutions and geography. As these change and evolve, so the composite energy and aura change and constructive growth inevitably ensues. For us human beings, our thinking and attitudes are vital components in the shaping of our environment and the way in which it in turn affects us and others.

It is interesting to note that Frankfurt, at the time of my observations, was about to be named the home of the European Bank, a fact reflected in the city's auric field — a questionable choice from a broad energy point of view. It will be interesting to observe how European finances unfold in the coming years. Furthermore, projects such as the implementation of a single European currency will only work well when the light and energy are right. Those involved have to look to their inner motives and determine what in their thinking they must change before such developments can be successful. A ray colour other than blue may be invoked, perhaps a deep violet which will precipitate more reflection and in turn compel the necessary changes in focus.

Cities, Towns and Auras

The study of the rays and their geographical locations is fascinating, not simply as an exercise in perception, but because we can become more aware of the nature of our own community and attune to its light and energy, its heart and soul, and thus work with it more creatively.

Towns, villages and other communities each have their own identity and aura. Studying them is a useful, perhaps essential, tool that the planners of the future can use as they consider ideas and seek to make decisions in everyone's interest.

I have used this process to view factories, banks, houses, shops and all manner of institutions to gain a view of their current effectiveness and their potential. Occasionally, I have been involved successfully, for example, in the recruitment of suitable staff appointed to turn around the fortunes of a company that is failing, or in considering the suitability of premises for a particular purpose.

Munich

As a comparison, I later travelled to Munich to lecture and teach. The vision of light around Munich was altogether different to that of the bustling commercial centre of Frankfurt. In the city's aura, there was a bright primrose yellow light, revealing the pursuit of excellence and intellectual and scientific interests, and a deep blue ray showing some reflective, almost mystical, energy. The dominant purple-violet ray gave the city an interesting cultural and spiritual quality, showing tendencies towards the arts, spiritual ideas and the broadening of the imagination. This makes Munich an engaging and stimulating place to visit and to live in and it also creates a village-like atmosphere. It is easy to feel at home in Munich, especially if you have opened up your spirit a little.

London

The aura of London, on my last visit, revealed complex auric pattern, probably because of the city's blend of small towns and villages that have progressively merged into one mass; all the edges have been blurred over time. But London has a unified field of its own in which its community lives, breathes and grows.

The dominant ray in London was the powerful emerald green of growth and change. It suggests that London is due for a gradual but nonetheless fundamental change to its role. I suspect this may be economic as well as cultural as the UK increasingly accedes to its European connections and the influences they bring.

In the future, London may well increase its role as a centre of innovation and fresh ideas, or at least, their implementation, but, of course, this would result in people's lives changing. London also influences the rest of UK and this desire for change has influenced parliament as successive governments have passed legislation for much radical change, not only for London, but

Auras and Colours

for the whole of the nation. With Welsh and Scottish assemblies and parliaments, this also heralds change in London's role — inherent in the light of the emerald ray.

The strong violet in the city's aura reiterates the increase in cultural developments and greater artistic significance in future times.

Your own town or city

It is possible to tune into your own town, city or village to perceive its aura and light.

Exercise 18

1. Still yourself with the clearing and radiating exercise.
2. Next, think of your city, town or village and, if possible, look across its skyline, noticing the buildings that give it its own distinctive character.
3. Remember all communities, as with individuals, have their angels and ask them for help in perceiving and viewing the rays emanating from the heart of your community as its aura, its field of light.
4. With your eyes open or closed, allow a simple, clear vision to appear, showing the auric field radiating in rainbow-like form, over your town, city or village.
5. Mentally note the colours (you will probably see at least two, or maybe three) in the order they are shown to you.
6. Remembering your community is a living entity in which you exist and participate, sense what the colours are saying to you.
7. Always be constructive in your conclusions and realisations. All communities have their problems and apparent drawbacks, but they also are vibrant with possibilities and you being there, being constructive in your ideas and actions, makes an enormous difference. Seek the good things, the creative, in all you view. That is the intuitive way.

8. Give thanks for your experience — with practice, you will see and understand more and more.

Buildings and Auras

The next time you visit an old building, whether it is a church, castle or other old site, just rest and be still within its walls for a while. Sit quietly and close your eyes. Then simply feel the place. Let your heart open and connect with the power and light of the building. Immerse yourself in its energy.

Remember that, like you, the building has an aura, a layer of subtle forces, which are a part of its being. It may not have a nervous system as you do, but it has a field of sensitivity with which you can empathise and have a dialogue. If you open your heart and mind, together, you will feel it, hear it and see it.

When a building has disappeared, for whatever reason, it leaves behind energy residues that can be seen and sensed for a long time afterwards. You can use yourself and your whole energy system as a magic wand to touch and experience these forces. The science fiction writer, Nigel Kneale, who wrote *The Quatermass Experiment*, also wrote an interesting play called *The Stone Tapes* in which researchers sought to record the messages left by antiquity in the stones of ancient ruined buildings — a kind of technical equivalent to the psychometry used by some mediums and psychics to read the images in the aura of an object.

Exercise 19

1. Take yourself off to the site of an old building or ruin, where in places at least, nothing is left of upper structures, the walls, towers and so on.
2. After clearing and radiating your aura, walk through the ruins, moving slowly and deliberately.
3. Focus your mind for a few moments on the idea of the

building as it was in its heyday. Let your imagination loose and enjoy yourself.

4. You may begin to see and view where walls or structures used to be, or at least, as I often do, see the energy patterns or aura they have left behind.

   These are often visible as glistening white-blue shadows or outlines, appearing to shimmer as they reveal the earlier form. For, although the stones, bricks and mortar may have disappeared, the energy that supported them will still be in place, at least in part.

5. As you walk around, the electromagnetic flow in your spine, like a magic wand, will help you to sense the energy and auric fields in the ruins.

   When you walk over old footings and through spaces where walls once stood, you may experience a rocking sensation, or a tingling in your hands; maybe a turning motion in your solar plexus, or the hair standing up on the back of your head. Enjoy it and note where it was so you can investigate further when you have finished.

6. Sometimes, such exercises can create 'headiness' or slight disorientation in very sensitive individuals. If this happens, simply breathe deeply, slowly and rhythmically, focusing on your solar plexus as you do so. In a few seconds everything will be back to normal. (Gently rubbing or stretching out your legs and feet will also help to ground you.)

7. Conclude by clearing and radiating your light.

Using this approach you can gradually attune to the building and its energy and you will find what you are looking for:

~ the location of walls or structures, long since gone from view

~ the voice and energy of the building, what it says to you about its history, its feel, its memory

~ the discarnate entities still connected to the building through their earthly memories.

At the end of such activity and after clearing and radiating energy as usual, always offer a blessing, such as the one suggested below, to the building and its invisible guardians. Some buildings need healing, but this should not be engaged in by a novice and should only be done by an experienced healer. Even some well-meaning attempts at deliverance rites in such circumstances can simply disrupt the energy rather than clear it.

Blessing

Through my heart, I bless this precious place in God's universe.
May it be full of light, peace and joy as the angels gather within its
walls. I thank the guardians and angels of this place for allowing me
the privilege of touching its soul and guiding my search.
So it is. Amen

Psychometry

Every time we touch an object, whether it is animal, vegetable or mineral, we influence the aura of the object by depositing some of our own energy and thought forms in its auric field, and we also affect our own.

Psychometry is the ability of a psychic to hold an object and read its history and sometimes, through the object, to link to the aura of its owner or former owners. I never psychometrise any object given to me at random as I do not regard any of my capabilities as a party trick. However, for the purposes of this book and as part of the unfoldment of your psychic mechanism, it is a valid exercise to try and to test.

Exercise 20

Take an object from a friend or relative and place it near you. You can choose a ring, a pen, a piece of jewellery, anything they have touched often that holds a lot of their thought forms and memories. It is also interesting to use a family heirloom, such as a pocket watch, where some of its history is known to the owner, but not to you.

1. Relax and bless the object, perceiving its aura to be full of light.
2. Clear and radiate your energy.
3. Lift the object and hold it gently in your hands.

    Be aware that you will primarily be working with three major chakras — the brow, the solar plexus and the heart centres.
4. Relax and ask the object to speak to you. The nerve centres in your hands and fingers will send information to the major centres along your spine and central nervous system.

    Imagine the dialogue commencing and travelling through your hands and arms to your heart, solar plexus and brow centres. With your solar plexus, feel and sense what the object is telling. With your heart, open to the joy of the memories it holds and those it is connected to. With your brow, allow the images to form, moving slowly across the picture screen inside your head.
5. Enjoy the experience and either tell the owner of the object what information the object shares with you, or record it for them if they are not with you, so that you may discuss it later.
6. Bless the object and return it to its owner. Clear and radiate your light, and return to normal awareness.

If this approach appeals to you, then practise it and research it further.

Energistics in Enterprise

I find I receive an increasing number of requests for consultations from people in business and those with high public profiles and that my services are often recommended by one to another.

I had helped Martin initially overcome his sorrow at his brother's suicide by making contact with his brother's higher mind and soul, and subsequently gave him some useful business advice.

A business acquaintance of his came to see me with his wife. Richard and Sandra had two interesting aura readings and there follows an extract from a letter he sent some time later, edited with confidentiality in mind.

You may recall giving my wife and myself consultations last December. We enjoyed meeting you and hearing what you had to say. I said to Sandra as we listened to the tapes on the way back to our home that I thought it had been a powerful experience. I still think this of our meeting.

It will probably come as no surprise to you that much has happened — you said 1995 would be a bit frantic — but despite much added stress and disruption to our lives, we are generally feeling very positive about everything.

When we saw you I was entrenched in my news company in London, although a Brussels-based company was showing some interest in me. You saw the Brussels prospect, much to my surprise, but the picture you painted about what could happen with this prospect, were I to go for it, was somewhat different to the one Sandra and I envisioned at the time. So different in fact that over the following few months I became, with apologies, doubtful about the veracity of your insights. However, we are now living, and I am working, in Brussels. It took longer to transpire than we had been expecting in December last year, but let's hope this is one of those cases where good things are worth waiting for.

You saw me commuting between Brussels and London, which I did not foresee. I had thought, should I ever get an offer, there would be an orderly transfer and that my family and I would move simultaneously. This proved impossible and indeed I commuted in and out of Heathrow almost weekly for seven weeks before the family joined me here.

More significantly at different points during the consultation you said that my sister, Mary, who passed over recently, was very keen for us to make this move and separately you suggested that some anniversaries in April and in May/June time might in some way tie in with the decision to move to Brussels.

At the time I really didn't know what significance any anniversaries would have. However, coincidentally, I received the job offer from my new employer on 14 April, the date of Mary's birthday — and my last official day with my London employer was 19 May, the anniversary of Mary's passing in 1993. I started with my new employer at midnight on 20 May and in fact was in Brussels at a ball that they had co-sponsored on 19 May.

It is certainly exciting and stimulating to meet and advise those in influential positions, but at the same time it can be a little disconcerting.

I have never claimed that my insights are infallible or that, as a healer, I could 'cure' everyone. The degree of spiritual perfection needed for such powers would make physical incarnation on earth unlikely, and unnecessary, as the greatest human lessons of self-knowledge and self-mastery would already have been accomplished. However, with the proviso that I can sometimes assist in the decision-making process, though without being solely responsible for the choices governing a large organisation, I am happy to test my vision and insights in this particular arena.

I began by perceiving the energy and light fields of individual managers, directors and so on but discovered I could often see beyond this level and interpret the energy field of an institution or corporation. This was an exciting development with huge implications.

Just as a human being, an animal, a tree or flower is contained within a beautiful coloured aura or energy field, so too is a factory, office or even football club! And that 'greater aura', as I term it, is a composite, built from the energies of all its constituent parts — not only the manager and staff but, perhaps surprisingly, the products or services as well. This has a far-reaching implication, for it means that the energy fields of those things we create has a separate life of its own and can influence the long-term prosperity of a business or institution and its participating employees.

There is also the energy of the building to consider and the location in which the institution resides. All these things together produce a fascinating web of possibilities, very complex yet vibrant, alive and accessible. From this intricate mix of light, energies and forces, the mind and soul of a company is born, sustained and ultimately ended.

Businesses and their light

Currently, I am involved as a consultant working for some international companies, assisting them in their decision- and policy-making. While my brief is very broad and I can be asked to give advice and insights on a wide range of issues or ideas concerning a company's future and development, there are fundamentally three modes or levels of perception I use.

When advising on the suitability of employees or candidates for a particular position in a company, I simply view the individual aura and chakras and make an assessment in the usual way.

Looking at company or institutional development requires that I view the aura of the company and its constituent parts to identify problem areas and the development stage of each unit. In Figure 12, 'A' is the head office or main centre of the business. As policy-making source it has to express creative, yet

A = HQ of company
B = Company seeking merger
1-4 = Subsidiary companies/units of A

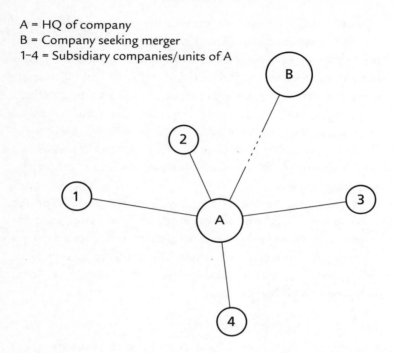

Figure 12 Constituent parts of a large company.

well-ordered energies. No imagination at 'A' means ultimate failure. The numbered circles 1-4 are the other units or aspects of the business; in a multinational, for example, they would be the foreign subsidiaries.

In this way it is possible to view a company's structure and the different levels of activity and stages of development of each constituent part. It is never healthy or indeed desirable that all the units of the company have the same aura, or express them-selves through the same energies. Just as the human body requires different organs, so the commercial company needs a body blended from different, but compatible, components. The cords that link the unit give an indication of the balance between the different units. Where this approach can be more effective than conventional analysis of such dynamics is in the capacity of auric energies to reveal otherwise invisible trends long before they become apparent at other levels, and also, perhaps more important, hidden opportunities and where and how they might arise.

I once told a manufacturing company to look to the USA for future business and cooperation. My insight and advice was met with a mixture of puzzled surprise and doubt that such a development was at all likely or viable. That was a few years ago and the company has since been approached by one American company with whom it now has a healthy agreement for manufacturing and distribution cooperation with others in the pipeline. I know its USA business will grow enormously if they follow their leads and keep a good vision; it could be a significant part of company turnover in years to come.

This brings us to the relationship between 'A' and 'B'. Company 'B' is seeking a merger with company 'A'. Here I would view this relationship in terms of compatibility. Whilst the company directors and managers explore the economics and other practical logistics of such a prospect, I view the prospective relationship of two dynamic entities. I can usually gain insight as to the long-term desirability of links between the two, though primarily from company 'A''s point of view, also considering the interests of 'B'. The company aura can show this, for at this level, what is ultimately right and good for one business, is also good for the other. The whole notion of competition changes when looking at life's possibilities this way.

Another important dynamic is that of owner and business (see Figure 13). Often the business and the owner will have a symbiotic, heart-based, relationship, the company energy and vision being largely that of the owner, and the two must be viewed together. If the owner's attitudes and focus are faulty or

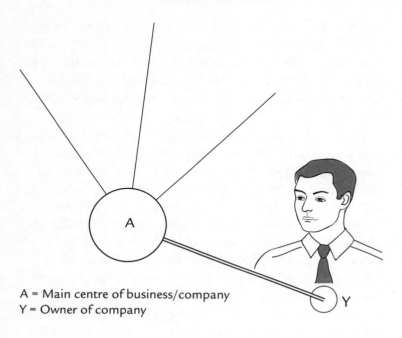

A = Main centre of business/company
Y = Owner of company

Figure 13   Heart-based relationship between owner and business.

weak, then this will be reflected in the company, and its employees will suffer. It will be a very frustrating company to work for and creative individuals will not stay long. Equally, where the owner or main force in the company is dynamic and creative, the company will flow while he or she flows along. The danger here is that the owner and the company are too interdependent.

This is where 'riding' a business is important. The owner stimulates and oversees the energy and progress of the business, but doesn't get too 'stuck' inside it. He or she incorporates the energies of others effectively within the business, using their imaginative and creative flair through the process of delegation and freedom linked to responsibility. The company would include personnel who can share some of the owner's role, so that he or she has space to grow and change. Conversely, the company would also have people who are able to perform the tasks that the owner is not able to do and, while sharing an empathy with the owner on overall principles, they would also think laterally using their innovative capacities. Studying aura can provide very useful insights into this process.

The third main area of perception I commonly use is in the exploration of the energy of a product or service. Strange as it may seem, products, artefacts and even services have energy fields.

Sometimes, just by studying brochures, I can see what products work well, which ones may struggle to be successful and what modifications may be needed. Those I work with will often give me technical brochures of their latest products. The technical data usually means nothing to me, but I may be able to see where a problem may be found or how something may be improved.

Recently, studying the aura of a chemical compound widely used in the pharmaceutical industry, I was able to diagnose, in layman's language, the nature of the weakness of the product and improvements that could be made. The compound was essentially sound, but needed to be adapted before it would do the job it had been developed to do. It will be successful, but only with the necessary modifications.

Patterns and cycles

It is also possible to develop ways of perceiving energy flow for an organisation or business, just as we can with an individual, to reveal optimum times at which to try to do things.

In Figure 14, a (very simple) sample movement or cycle change is shown. It shows a view of energy flow indicating that, until the end of the month of April, there is good potential for change, growth and innovation and then the establishment of equilibrium. This is because the green ray is in dominance. As we move into May, a new energy (blue) takes precedence and tends to create a less action-packed, more reflective time — a time for expansive thinking, originality and vision and ideas for future developments.

In business, this would suggest that the period to the end of April is good for changing staff and introducing new products or services, while the period immediately following gives the chance to look ahead again and find inspiration for the next set of creative possibilities for the company, as well as time for the unfoldment and development of effective communication and good marketing (assuming it is the right kind of blue).

Such a view does not suggest that change can only occur at certain times, it simply indicates the times when such change may be easier to precipitate and effect. The shaded area is a crucial period of crossover, sometimes a little unsettling for those involved and usually requiring a special alertness in the company, especially at management level. It can also be very exciting, full of activity and expectancy.

A period influenced predominantly by the yellow ray (not shown) would have been mostly a time for practical planning issues to be considered, such as re-tooling, new campaigns, or strategies being checked and finalised.

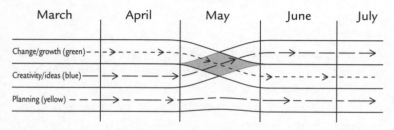

Figure 14 A simple cycle change illustration.

When we seek to initiate change, it is sometimes frustrating because we are trying to achieve a particular goal at times which are not the most appropriate. It is not always easy to remember that a little patience and willingness to wait will eventually lead to a more suitable time in which to implement fresh ideas and plans. It is just a question of timing — and the light can show us which time is best.

Ley Lines

As a young boy, I had many visions that revealed bands of coloured light stretching across the earth's surface. Later, I stumbled across a book on ley lines by Alfred Watkins and this enabled me to unlock my understanding of this phenomenon. These bands or streams of energy, predominantly blue or orange-red in colour, I could see to be the lines Watkins described — the nervous system of our planet. What began to fascinate me was how we, as human beings, were influenced by this network and how we could tap into it consciously. These were the secrets of the ancient ones who knew how to benefit from the hidden power and the force lines of the earth. They knew how we could live in harmony with the earth.

This is an important idea. I learned that we are here to be at one with the earth and its energy forces and to work in tune with the patterns it creates for our mutual benefit.

The planet is governed by its own great intelligence, far superior to anything we can conceive. Contrary to the sense of doom that accompanies concerns over pollution and the apparent destruction we are causing, I believe that we can never even begin to control or destroy the earth; it is only man's ego that makes him believe he can. My insights and experience have taught me that many of the conditions we see as problems that we cause — climate changes, ozone depletion and so on — are part of a controlled plan that the planet understands very well.

It is our responsibility to develop a deep empathy and dialogue with the earth and its energies. Animals are fully attuned to these forces; birds and dolphins navigate around the planet, with the leys as points of reference to which they connect via their pineal centre, giving them bearings and guidance.

Altering the paths of ley lines, and practices such as 'earth acupuncture', where people try to shift or 'purify' the earth's energies, cannot be achieved. Such changes can never be permanent if the planet (as is usual) does not wish it; in time, the movement of these forces returns to where the earth desires. New Age practices which claim to 'switch on' chakras in the earth or, using crystals and iron bars, divert ley lines that interfere with our sleep because they are found to flow through our homes, are futile. Our role is attunement and co-operation, not manipulation.

These lines of force, whose network exists at many levels of intensity, are neither good nor bad. Usually, we are only subconsciously aware of the forces, and ignorance of them is generally the key component in difficulties we experience with roads or buildings. When we move across the lines or walk along them, our own state of awareness can be affected in different ways. Therefore, when building roads, for example, a knowledge of the local lines can help in preventing the creation of mysterious accident black spots, or it can encourage a balanced and welcoming atmosphere in a building.

As with all life, ley lines have different polarities, positive and negative, just as we do in our bodies, to provide balance and sustain equilibrium.

The earth's chakras, or nerve plexi, are linked by the major ley lines as they work their way across the planet's surface, inside the planetary aura, the female negatively charged lines curving around and sometimes criss-crossing the more direct, male lines (see Figure 15). As well as negative and positively

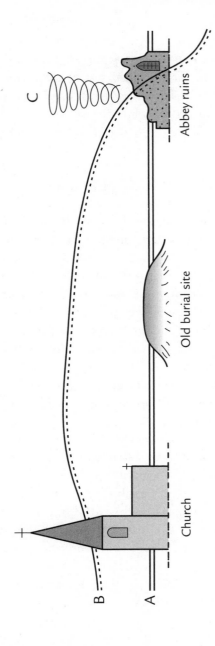

Figure 15 Ley lines and energy centres — the earth's nervous system.

A = Male (positive) ley line
B = Female (negative) ley line
C = Energy vortex/chakra, where lines cross.

Nerve centres

Ley lines do not run perfectly straight, as some suggest, but actually bend and twist across the earth's surface, linking the nerve centres that naturally occur in the planetary energy or etheric body along the planet's surface. This nervous system corresponds to the chakras and meridians found in the energy or etheric bodies of all living entities.

---

charged lines, there are also integrated lines that are a blend of both polarities — neutral lines in effect.

The Rod of Caduceus, symbolically depicting the serpent energy crossing back and forth on its winding path over the central column of the spinal nerves, visually illustrates the effect of the major lines, twisting and turning, bringing balance to the space around them. In any dwelling or building, both male and female types of line will be found as well as, occasionally, the neutral leys. Most, if not all, sacred and significant buildings were placed by our wiser ancestors on the points where the earth's major ley forces cross creating energy centres. The famous, male, Michael line runs through the abbey ruins in my home town of Bury St Edmunds, accompanied by its female, or negatively polarised, companion, the Mary line.

From the major lines, smaller ones radiate, forming an elaborate network of force lines across the whole planet. These are the branch lines radiating from the main network structure. It is possible to tune into ley lines very easily, or at least to spot them in your own area. If you have a room for healing, meditation or similar practices in your home, it will make a link via one of the branch lines from that room to the nearest major ley line.

Many people use pendulums, dowsing rods and so on to find ley lines and often enough it is effective, but my experience

Finding ley lines — dowsing

There are many methods we can use to find ley lines by dowsing. I have watched people dowsing, using metal rods or pendulums of various kinds, with much success and reasonable accuracy. My own neighbour, a senior hospital consultant with no more than a passing interest in his friend's strange work, discovered such an ability in himself a few years ago when his young son found a pair of dowsing rods among his birthday presents. He was very surprised to discover an energy line between our two properties, which travels across our road into an adjacent street.

On one occasion when I was teaching in Edinburgh, a city full of beautiful forces and ideas, I mentioned to the students that I could see these force lines. As always in such circumstances, I was challenged, albeit in a light-hearted fashion, to demonstrate where these lines travelled through the building we were using. The twinkle in the eye of the young man who asked me betrayed a deeper understanding than he had so far revealed.

I walked across the room, showing where the force lines were (I later established that they came from the direction of the castle, which was to be expected) and also where a significant spiral of light came up from the earth into the centre of the room. The man smiled and said to me, 'That is exactly where they were dowsed by Sheriff Middleton.'

Sheriff Middleton was a well-respected dowser in Scotland and his description of the lines coincided exactly with my vision. (I must say I was relieved to discover this as, however much we believe what we see and know, a challenge can easily affect one's confidence!)

suggests that using our subtle vision is far more revealing and comprehensive and is worth the patience and effort to unfold it. It is a natural part of your perception that has simply been dormant and needs gentle, gradual awakening.

Ley-spotting

Do these exercises on a nice, calm, warm day if outside. It will be easier to relax, and the energies, both in you and the earth, are more vibrant. Try to use a rural or pastoral space where the earth's surface is in view. The exercises can be done effectively anywhere, even in a city centre or park, but the frequencies in quiet, natural spaces lend themselves better to this type of activity.

Don't forget to do the clearing and radiating exercise before and after these activities.

Ley-spotting with maps
Exercise 21

1. Find a local ordnance survey map and place it on a table in front of you.
2. Look for the following buildings or sites:
~ churches, religious buildings or sites
~ ruined antiquities such as abbeys, cathedrals, castles
~ ancient sites, standing stones, barrows, burial mounds and old earthworks such as dykes
~ old inns or public houses
~ other significant buildings such as halls, mansions or stately homes.

   Put small pencil circles around the ones you feel are significant, those that in some way seem to draw your attention.
3. Give a blessing to the map and the district or area it represents, for it is both a mirror of it and access point to it, a window through which the light may be seen.
4. Through your heart, ask the earth to show its magnificent network of light and the lines along which its power flows. Then relax and look at the map as though you are looking

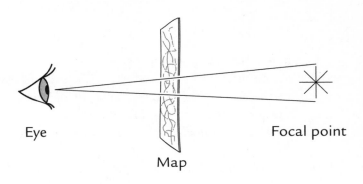

Eye   Focal point

Map

Figure 16 Ley-spotting using a map.

through it, with your focal point a little beyond the map's surface (see Figure 16).

5. Gradually, as you scan it, the map will reveal to you the earth's energy pattern in a way you can recognise. For me, it quite clearly shows the lines in distinctive colour frequencies — red/orange for the predominantly positively charged line and turquoise/blue for the negatively charged ones. A neutral, integrated line shows green.

Your perception may be a little different to mine and you may have a different coding, but trust what you are shown and note it down, drawing the lines on the map.

With time, practice and patience, you will be surprised at what you see, and the way the line movements link many of the sites and buildings you have selected. Once you have explored your own area, look elsewhere to deduce the major ley line systems. And then see if you can walk along them. There will often be old tracks or roads along some of their route, and maybe dykes or footpaths. You will feel the power flow up and down your spine as you do so.

Ley-spotting outdoors

Exercise 22

1. Select another beautiful place or location to visit as before. Make it a space that is as 'open' as possible — a park, or fields, or perhaps the grounds of a stately home or old building. Find somewhere your heart feels drawn to.

2. Allow yourself to be guided to a peaceful, tranquil corner or spot where you have a good view of the location, somewhere you feel particularly comfortable. When you have found it, call on the spiritual guardians of the place in a brief, silent prayer and thank them for helping you.

3. Then relax deeply into the feel of the place. Smell its perfumes, feel its sensations, its true connections, and hear the sounds. Soak up the wonderful quality of the location and let it truly link with you. Enjoy a kind of reverie, calm and relaxed.

4. Ask the place to reveal to you its patterns of light and energy. (It may already have begun to do so.) And trust what you see. You will feel the place in your solar plexus and your inner eye (head centres) will show you exactly what you need to see.

5. Sometimes, by closing your eyes, you may be able to view more easily at first, the picture and structures your inner vision is trying to unfold for you.

6. Say thank you when you have finished, even if, as is possible in the early attempts, you may think you have experienced very little.

Water and Light

When we moved into our present house, about ten years ago, my wife suggested that we had a pond, so I dug one in the top corner of our garden, my 'Zen corner', as I now call it, and it is thriving. Several generations of fish have been born in it, the flowers around it bloom and a host of pond life has taken up residence, including several frogs.

At night time especially, the light of the water devas or sprites can be seen. Over the top of the pool there appears a canopy of transparent white energy. In and around this light, other star-like coloured forms move and pause; these are the elementals that work through water, ponds, rivers and streams and even oceans. Their role is to ensure the continued natural patterns and cycles within the water as it transforms and evolves from liquid through force to particles and then back to liquid again.

Sitting peacefully near to a pool or river, you can't fail to at least feel their presence. Enjoy it.

Trees, Flowers and Plants

Trees, flowers, plants and indeed all things have auras and subtle fields. In fact, all physical and three-dimensional realities are the dense, material manifestation of subtle fields.

I love to spend time in my garden on sunny days; the beautiful light radiating from nature has a wonderful healing effect, especially on the emotional self. I sit quietly and attune to the flowers and shrubs, especially around the pond. Have you noticed how, if you move forward to smell the scent of a flower, it offers its energy to you and, as it does, the perfume increases, becoming more intense, more powerful?

Sit and look at your own garden, or the surrounding vegetation — the trees, flowers and wondrous natural abundance around you. Bless it, give thanks for it and then relax back and allow visions of its aura to form.

It may appear as misty cloud-like radiations around the flowers, leaves or trees, or as a more dynamic, coloured auric field. Just relax and enjoy it, emphasising your oneness and connection with this life.

You may also behold the coloured 'fairy lights' that you almost certainly saw in your childhood, and that I mentioned earlier in this book. These are the lights or forces of the elementals, the fairies or nature spirits that work in the natural world, encouraging the flow of the cycles of life. They are related to the angelic realms and sometimes appear in personified form — they may do that for you. Thank them for being there.

The energy field of seeds
Exercise 23

1. For this exercise, take a large flower seed (or plant bulb) and place it on a table before you.
2. After briefly doing the clearing and radiating exercise, bless the seed and the life forces that it represents. Try to be aware of the elementals of the angelic kingdom and ask them to assist you in your endeavours.
3. Relax and gaze at the seed, recognising the energy it possesses and the complex information it contains that will enable it to grow into a flower.
4. As you rest and attune, you may begin to perceive the aura that permeates it and radiates around it, like a beautiful halo.

    This may initially reveal itself as a rather smoky white-blue cloud. After a time and a little persistence, you will begin to see the blue intensify and other colours appear, especially silver-white, yellow and rose-red.

Practise, give yourself time and you will see. Always give thanks when you have finished.

This simple exercise will help you to attune to all the beautiful vitalities and light of all trees and flowers and natural things. It is the beginning of a dialogue with them and they will respond to you (and grow more beautifully) the more you attune to them, bless them and affirm your oneness with them.

This approach is very much that used by Dr Rudolph Steiner in his work, *Knowledge of Higher Worlds*.

Planets, Suns and Solar Systems

Our planet earth is a living being. The ancients understood this. As part of the New Age awakening that is taking place, one of the better ideas to emerge is that relating to the Gaia awareness, the Mother Earth teachings. Here, we are departing from the idea of the planet as some mineral clump, floating around in space, there to be exploited and polluted at man's convenience.

Instead, we are beginning to see the planet through our hearts, as well as our heads and with that comes the inevitable realisation of the earth as a living, breathing being, the physical manifestation of a great soul and spirit in its own right.

All our own human nature and being operates within this planet's framework while we are alive upon it. The earth in turn is an integral feature of our solar system and its light and nature. Just as we exist and have our physical and three-dimensional experience through the planetary body, so our planet has its experience through the solar body, of which it is a part. This mystical truth is then reflected first through constellations, then galaxies and ultimately, universes.

Our physical and etheric nature are loaned from the planet and, on physical 'death', we relinquish those aspects of ourselves. But we retain, for a time at least, much of the astral or emotional self until we have processed the emotional experiences of our lifetimes. This emotional self is also linked to the earth, which has its own kind of emotional field or aura (see Figure 17).

Around the earth is a mental field in which our mind operates, that is, the concrete mind and the abstract mental self. And the earth is ensouled, in other words, has a soul self, an individual spiritual self, just as we do.

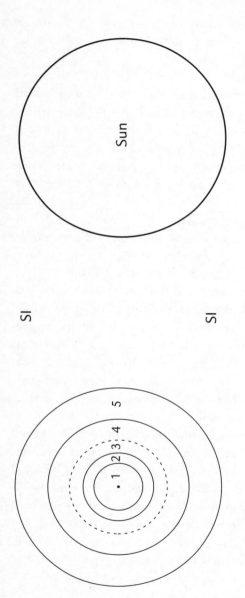

SI = Integrated solar plane (sun's soul plane) encompassing whole solar system

1 = Physical earth
2 = Etheric/energy field of earth
3 = Emotional/astral plane of earth
4 = Mental planes of earth
5 = Soul plane of earth

Figure 17 The earth's aura.

In turn, all these planetary selves, manifesting as auras, exist with the sun's aura or solar light and planes. Our spirit, our essence, embraces all these things and is universal, not limited to a particular system or planet. To an extent, this is also true of our soul self and its light, though some of our soul nature is 'borrowed' from within the earth's soul plane and some pertains to the sun's soul plane and in turn, that of the universe.

Light of the world

We can connect with our planet and, through it, with its link with the sun. It is our light within the earth's aura that is most significant in that respect.

Exercise 24

1. Relax, breathe deeply and clear and radiate your energy.
2. Remember how you exist at so many levels. Some are visible in your aura. Think of them now as they radiate into the space around you: your etheric self through which you experience power and energy; the vibrant astral or emotional self, that irridescent layer of fast moving colour and light in which you feel and can attain such beautiful, heart-centred feelings; the brilliant mental self, from where your thoughts filter through, dominated by wondrous, almost indescribable yellow, gold, turquoise and rose light; the plane of the mind; and your soul self, your doorway to the spirit, the magnificent spiritual you that connects you with your wisdom, your destiny.
3. All these levels and more exist in you and around you as you celebrate yourself. Sense yourself to be in the centre, radiating all these remarkable lights, and let the image grow in your inner eye, in the picture box of your mind.
4. Now, as the pineal centre does its work, allow yourself to fly high above the earth. You see the earth, a beautiful, blue

planet wrapped in a quilt of majestic white clouds.

5. And then the earth radiates its own magnificence for you. It shows you its light, its aura. Thank the soul of the planet through which you are privileged to live this physical life. Thank it for revealing its magic to you. Let the pictures form; enjoy them.

6. Then imagine the solar system, set in a wondrous starry sky, our own sun wrapping its light and power around each planet in a kaleidoscope of caress and support. Here you are. Meditate on this. You live and dwell in the most beautiful place, an awesome universe.

7. And then remember the planets are physical manifestations of the solar chakras or centres of a great solar being. The sun is the heart centre. Hold this vision and idea in your mind and heart for a while.

8. Finally, come slowly back to earth. Reconnect gently with yourself here in the midst of earthly life, sustained, loved and inspired by the light of the universe, the galaxy, the solar system and our Mother Earth.

CHAPTER 6
LIGHTS BEYOND LIFE

Life seems more sweet that Thou didst live
And men more true that Thou wert one;
Nothing is lost that Thou didst give,
Nothing destroyed that Thou hast done.
Anne Brontë

As I drove towards Munich airport, I was thinking of my daughter, Ruth. The cab driver taking me to the airport was playing a cassette of the Mendelssohn violin concerto which Ruth loved and had played herself, so maybe that was the trigger that sent my mind away into such thoughts.

I'd had a busy two weeks working in Bavaria and I was looking forward to getting home. The flight was quite full and I was enjoying a drink with my meal, chatting to the young businessman sitting next to me.

The drinks trolley was making a second run along the gangway and as it did so, my father, who had passed over some years earlier, appeared to me. I had decided not to have a second drink, but my father looked at me with an uncharacteristically serious gaze and pointed to the drink on my tray. 'Have another,' came the advice. I didn't need much persuading and I thought, 'Oh well, tomorrow is a day off, and I am being collected at the airport ... '

The reason for Dad's appearance eluded me but I didn't query it at all. After all, he always had liked a celebratory drink and he often appeared at significant times. 'You need it,' he murmured inside my head. 'Perhaps I do,' I mused.

Arriving at the airport, I was met by my wife and, surprisingly, my neighbour who is a doctor. My heart sank. Something was obviously wrong. It transpired that my daughter had been in a very serious road accident on the previous night and was lucky to have survived. My wife, brave as always, had decided not to try to contact me as I couldn't have returned any earlier and she saw no point in worrying me as Ruth would recover, despite serious injuries. My neighbour, who had been a marvelous help to my wife in the last few hours, refused to let my wife drive to collect me alone as she was exhausted. His medical knowledge and connections as a consultant at the hospital had been wonderfully applied, as had his care and friendship.

My father, or the soul who was my father in this lifetime, obviously felt a need to touch my mind and heart at this time of great difficulty to reassure me — and to have a second brandy had been sound advice!

At another time, I was in Seattle talking with a middle-aged American lady. She had some difficult decisions to make and felt quite alone in dealing with them. Quite suddenly, there was an image of her deceased husband, around whom some of her concerns were centred.

He appeared in the Air Force uniform he used to wear years ago, and gave her assurances that what she was seeking to do at that time could work through perfectly well. She was comforted and felt enormously supported by his light and the presence of his soul.

As he took his leave from us, he told me that there was a photograph of him dressed in the military uniform he was wearing that day (this is quite a common phenomenon in such situations). His wife Kathy had some difficulty with that idea. 'I have no photos of him dressed like that,' she said.

A few days later, she received a letter through the post from the sister of her late husband. Included with the letter was a photograph of Kathy's husband in his service uniform, just as he had appeared to us that afternoon. Her sister-in-law had been clearing through some drawers and had discovered the photo of her brother by chance; she felt Kathy would like it.

Furthermore, the postmark on the envelope was the same as the date of our meeting — a useful indicator that those souls living in the light beyond this life are able to have a caring connection with us and can touch our lives in this dimension.

Death

It is generally believed that all our fears, everything that causes us anxiety, has its roots in our fear of death. My experience, like that of many others, suggests that death, certainly in the sense of the ultimate human dénouement, is a fiction believed by those who have been successfully conditioned culturally to accept the single belief that 'if you can't touch it, it doesn't exist.' Scientists spend so much time looking for 'proof'.

But, the physicist Professor Arthur Ellison said in a television interview, 'No one can actually prove anything to anyone else. The science of proof is a myth.' He went on to say, 'I cannot even prove I'm having this interview!'

Particle physics supports this idea increasingly. It has been found that sub-atomic particles modify their behaviour (and therefore the results of experiments), dependent on who is watching or observing them. The observer influences the observed. Thus, everything has a considerably more subjective quality than many of us previously realised.

Death is one such idea. Twentieth-century mediums and clairvoyants have also been caught up in seeking proof that the personality survives physical death. However, the simplistic model offered by such messages and communications that our mothers, fathers and so on, continue in another dimension as they did in this one, I'm afraid to say, is a delusion.

Euthanasia

I have no strong feelings about euthanasia, though my experience suggests it is an imperfect way to leave this world.

I base this upon two things. In my work as a healer I have noticed, where good supportive loving care is given to the one who is dying and effective healing and medical practice is used, a relatively peaceful transition can be achieved, often with a reduced need for medication. And having observed an induced death, I can assure the reader that, whatever the high motives of all involved, the higher bodies appear to detach through the solar plexus and as a result the individual experiences some temporary difficulty after passing that would not be the case if the heart or head (crown) were the focus.

Into the Afterlife

At death, the physical body is released by the soul, or the higher self. When the useful work of this lifetime is done and the physical body is no longer needed, over a period of some days, the higher — etheric or energistic; emotional or astral; and mental — bodies, all loosen their connections with the physical cells. These cells have been held in their positions in the physical body at various frequencies or resonances to form the organs, bones and tissues. When the release is completed, the physical body gradually disintegrates and it returns its atoms to the earth.

During this process, we can observe that these bodies appear to move away from the physical sheath, the main point of disconnection being a space close to the solar plexus chakra, the heart, or the crown of the head. The precise point of detachment depends on the evolution and mentality of the individual and also the nature of the passing or death.

Modes of passing

Emotionally centred people, with extremely strong emotional ties, tend to detach from a point near to the solar plexus centre. This is seen less and less at this time, but it is a reason why those of us left behind must release people emotionally so that they can go on their next journey when the time comes. Our emotional tugging at them can be a problem. I believe this is why so often a passing occurs just after family and close friends have left the bedside of the one who is dying — it is simply easier for them. This is precisely what my own mother did as I had left her bedside only a short time before she passed on and left her physical body.

When my mother-in-law was dying, my father-in-law was quite naturally distressed and in turmoil at the prospect of the love of his life leaving him so young, only fifty-five years old. She said to my wife, her eldest child, 'I wish Dad would let me go.'

At the point of death, many souls detach through the space near the heart centre. This enables a smoother, less emotional farewell. I am not suggesting we should not have feelings at the passing of a loved one or that we should not feel sorrow or shed tears, for that is the way our human nature has developed and how we are conditioned.

But as we become more enlightened, more aware, we truly understand that passing out of physical consciousness and earthly body is merely a stage of development, not unlike the birth with which we enter this life. Once we have rediscovered how to prepare for our death and the next part of the eternal journey, then our whole perspective will shift as we realise we 'lose' no one, it is simply that our relationship with them changes and moves on.

Solar plexus deaths tend to leave us heavily connected to our emotional natures in the next awareness, the next life. We don't want to let go; our emotional affection we call love wants us to hold on.

But heart centre passing leaves us in a much calmer reality and tranquil mode. When the heart rules, we love, but are willing to release the one dying to go on their way. We realise we cannot possess them, that they are a blessing to us and that true love unbinds, has no conditions, and sets us free.

Most of us leave through the space near to the heart or the crown of our heads as we die. This is why, so often just before death, people can appear to rally a little and generally perk up, even suddenly looking a little healthier and younger.

My grandmother, who had had a stroke and was seriously ill in hospital, suddenly seemed to be recovering and was sitting up in bed, and everyone thought how bright she looked. Shortly afterwards, she passed on.

This happens because we literally die from our feet upward. When our root centre finally 'closes down', this signals that we are about to leave the physical body. And as the higher energies rise upwards, towards the crown, we experience an increase in power and light around our upper bodies and finally, our heads, just preceding the final detachment and parting.

A good, loving and experienced healer should always be present to work with those who are dying. Just as we need energy to sleep, we need energy when dying, and the energy a healer brings to such a situation facilitates a more peaceful, beautiful passing. In my view, when a person is waiting to pass, the attendance of a healer, or a healing presence, whether they recognise themselves as such or not, is a desirable practice.

Always remember, death is merely a stepping through from one level of life to another — we all do it and I believe we have done it many times before.

Exercise 25
This is a good moment to pause and consider those we have known and loved and who have passed on to the higher life.

1. Go through the clearing and radiating exercise as usual.
2. When you can feel the stillness all around you, give thanks for all those you have known who have passed into the next life from this world and have blessed your life.
3. Give a few moments thought to those who have especially had a great impact upon your development as a human being, those who have taught you how to love, those who have inspired you, helped you, taught you patience and tolerance and perhaps even challenged you.
4. Give thanks to them all and be aware that they have gone nowhere, but have merely departed the scene, left the drama and are active in other levels or dimensions of themselves, living their existence through other realities, other worlds that are connected to our world here.
5. Consider the whole pattern, your birth, life and the birth into the next life we call death. See it as one journey going on forever.
6. Close by saying a little prayer of thanks for your own life here and ask for guidance so you may live your life fully and effectively as a tribute to those ancestors who have pathed the way and gone before you.

> *Divine love, help me to live my life fully, to serve, to give and*
> *to bear witness to the energy, love and light of those who*
> *trod this way before me.*

7. Bring yourself back to normal consciousness.

The Dream World

Our dreams are mini–death–experiences. Each night when we are asleep, our higher bodies or selves leave our physical body to rest and repair as it needs, and our focus moves to some of the planes close to the earth. We experience what is really a temporary death, from which we return when we wake. Our dreams

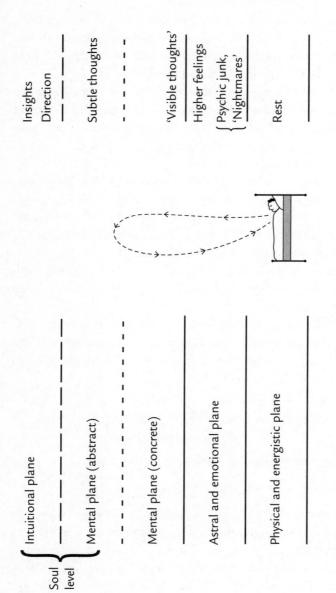

Figure 18 The dream journey.

170

are essentially a mixture of memories of that experience, and when we reconnect with our physical body after sleep, usually we retain a collection of very vivid images and thought forms from the lower astral plane (see Figure 18). In controlled dream investigation, it is possible to link with our experiences during sleep of the higher patterns beyond the psychic junk or flotsam of the lower astral plane and to develop a rapport with that part of higher dream activity.

It is important here to mention that, at this time of accelerating change on the earth, and also in each of us, dream patterns are changing. This is because the astral or emotional plane is experiencing a great healing as we progress towards emotionally clearer life patterns. The fear-laden thought forms that have dominated us for so long are being purged and our dreams are reflecting that process. Not only are many of us are experiencing more frequent, vivid, spontaneous dream recall, but our dreams are also tending to be less metaphorical, more literal, more direct and instructive.

It is very interesting to observe someone, especially a child, while they sleep. Of course, you should ask their permission first and obviously be very quiet and gentle.

I used to watch my own children when they were younger and I could see the gentle light appearing to be above the body, linking their physical home to their mental and soul nature very clearly. And the etheric body seems to become quite bright and almost crystal-like as it accelerates the healing and regeneration processes in the physical tissues. Much healing is possible at this time.

If you sit and relax and look at a child sleeping, you will undoubtedly sense, if not see, the beautiful light around them. And remember, all the different levels and bodies overlap and interact — the gap in our perception that conceals them from us is paper-thin and requires of us just a little adjustment in our awareness before we can perceive these other worlds of light.

Ghosts

After physical death, once the physical body has been vacated, our etheric or energy body remains for a while. I have seen the energy body of an individual, some months after physical passing, very much intact. On other occasions, this body appears to disintegrate very quickly, within days of death. The reasons for this are unclear to me, though I think it may have some link to the health and vitality of the individual while they are on earth.

Poor health can indicate a weakness in some level of the energy structure as well as a weak physical body. But some people build very powerful, healthy energy bodies while on earth, and they simply take longer to break down. This energy form, of smoky-white hue, will be magnetically attracted to those who have a connection to it or to locations it visited when it was attached to the physical body. As the connections with the emotional and mental bodies weaken after death, this body is no longer governed by the higher self or soul and can literally drift, like a balloon on the breeze, as it dissipates and crumbles away.

The sighting of many such ghosts and apparitions are the consequence of sudden sensitivity to these energy forms, often at a time of heightened awareness or emotional arousal.

Eventually, after death, our reality is focused in the astral realm and we live in the level of life we perceive a little through the aura, a world of bright powerful colours, strong images, governed much more directly by thought. As we think, we change. It is this self we seem to 'inhabit' after death and we use it to project back into this world our thoughts and ideas to those who are willing and able to listen.

Often this is done through the mind of a psychic, referred to as a medium. There are many mediums who deny they are psychics, in pursuit of elitism. In fact the mechanism is essentially the same, whether viewing an aura or perceiving and communicating with the minds and feelings of those no longer in physical mode. You cannot be mediumistic if you are not psychically awakened, and any psychic can work mediumistically; in either case, you are perceiving and attuning to the emotional and mental levels. Also, the law of attraction applies here and you attract according to the level and nature of your own mind and thinking.

Ultimately most, except those at the very lowest level of soul-development, relinquish their emotional vibration and body and become mental beings, linked to their souls. They then seek to understand the life they have had and work through the next part of their journey.

Ghost-busting

'We have been given your name, Sir,' the duty officer said rather apologetically, 'and it was suggested to us that you can sort out this kind of thing.'

'This kind of thing' involved the story of three very anxious young women, one of whom had had some remarkable experiences while driving along a local stretch of the A11. Her two friends confirmed her story as she began to unravel it for me in the lounge of my home one bright June evening.

A few years before, a very close friend of hers had been killed in an accident on this road and, recently, when travelling on the same stretch, she had experienced several extremely unusual phenomena.

Her car on each occasion would suddenly become very cold inside as they passed the location of the accident, as if a cool mist had suddenly descended. Simultaneously, the steering would start to go out of control, and the headlights would enter a rapid flashing sequence, going from very dim to excessively bright and all levels in between.

This had not only terrified the lady, Mrs McDonald, but also the police who had witnessed the incredible light display, and the garage

---

who subsequently examined the car and could find no fault with its electrical system. Mrs McDonald's friends were also very worried!

I decided to accompany them one evening. As the light was fading, we could test the headlights. Her friends came along in the back of the car and I also asked along two friends of my own, who would follow in their car.

The journey went perfectly smoothly as we drove towards the A11. It was a pleasant evening, the sun setting through the trees. We turned onto the A11 and then ... all hell broke loose!

The energy patterns around Mrs McDonald were quite visible and they began to alter violently as we travelled over the accident spot. The car chilled a little inside. Next, the steering took on a life of its own as we wrestled to keep it on track. The A11 is a busy road, even at night, and not a road where anyone can afford to fool about. At one point, Mrs McDonald removed her hands from the wheel completely but somehow, the steering was being managed by invisible forces.

Finally, the light display started and we managed to pull the car over on to the grass beside the road. Cars coming towards us were pulling over and stopping, their occupants frozen in amazement at what they saw and we had to wave them on to avoid congestion and a possible accident. I felt that I was witnessing some exceedingly clever circus trick and expected the clowns to appear any minute.

It became obvious to me, however, that the problem was being caused by the driver herself. I could detect nothing unusual around us nor indeed could my sensitive friend who had travelled behind us.

But Mrs McDonald, with her natural sensitivity, awareness and high energy levels, was somehow affecting the car as her memories and consequent thoughts triggered this amazing activity in her emotional body and aura. It was a series of rapid electrical flashes from her aura that interfered with the car's normal activity, short-circuiting her car's electrics.

This type of experience has proved invaluable and has stood me in good stead over the years when being asked by police, the Citizens

Advice Bureau and others to help those who are encountering psy-cho-spiritual and phenomenal problems: it is not the phenomenon that should concern me, but the people who are in the centre of the experience. *They are the trigger. It also illustrates how we are vulnerable to our own fears, attracting them to us.*

All phenomena need a source of energy that will give power and the potential for physical, material manifestation. Without them nothing will happen. And while I agree that there are locations, buildings and so on, where the natural forces of the place are more likely to precipitate unusual, psychic experiences, especially in the sensitive individual, it is always the individual, initially at least, and not the site of the experience that needs attention and, usually, some kind of healing.

In this case, the process was triggered in Mrs McDonald as she crossed a powerful ley line. She was very sensitive and suffering a little from post-natal depression, a term used to describe the psychic centre and hormonal changes experienced by a woman after child-birth. The ley line traverses the road, temporarily affecting drivers, a notorious accident black spot.

Mrs McDonald received healing. The headlights ceased their merry dance and all quickly returned to normal. She was able to drive safely again, without fear of another frightening encounter.

Thought Forms and Astral Bodies

Many other ghosts are the astral bodies of departed individuals whose minds and souls no longer control or govern their actions. These astral bodies contain powerful thought forms and images, especially of the body image and appearance they had in their early life. These appear, once again, in places to which they are magnetically attracted by associations during the physical life or because they are drawn, as are all other thoughts, to those who are thinking in resonance or in harmony with them.

Sadly, many mediums and psychics give messages from those thought forms and astral entities, because they can seem to converse with us and give us information that we did not know. However, these thought forms and astral entities tend to be a little predictable. They will tend to go through the same kind of motions and patterns. Hauntings are usually manifest as variations around a theme, often in the same place, or walking the same path or route. Any dialogue with an astral entity no longer connected to its soul will tend to be banal, of a low level generally and repetitive.

To a psychically experienced person, the thoughts projected to us from a soul-governed mind on other planes is easy to distinguish from that of the thought form or astral entity. Its light is entirely different and in any true contact a departed entity will not be holding on to old prejudices from this life. It will not come through a medium or to you in a direct manner telling you how to live your life, what decisions to make, that it is angry with you or unhappy and so on. It will come simply to tell you that it loves you, perhaps to thank you and to encourage you to live through your heart. It may encourage you, but it will not tell you what to do. My father's light suggesting I have another brandy is one thing, but control and giving strict instruction is totally different.

It is a contravention of fundamental spiritual laws and should be ignored, wherever we are told it has emanated from.

Spirits

We are all spirits, in fact everything is made from different levels of spiritual substance, so to talk of a 'spirit world' is inaccurate. There is no such place and my understanding is that those who communicate through mediums from 'the other side' and refer continually to the 'spirit world' are either low-level entities not worth connecting with, or higher beings limited in the language they can use by the conditioned vocabulary in the medium's mind. All worlds are spirit worlds, including this one.

When we see or feel the presence of a loved one who has died, it may be simply a thought form. Equally, it can be the image they are building for us, so that we may recognise them for who they used to be. It is important for us to realise they are no longer the person we knew. Anyone who has had any kind of out-of-the-body experience or profound spiritual awakening will understand that. In the prelude to this book, I described the memory I have of my pre-birth experience and that we meet the person we are going to be, like a uniform we adopt for the life to come. On death, we give up that model, discard that uniform and become a creature of higher light. The images we project for the minds of those still on the earth are, of necessity, ones they will recognise, so we show them who we used to be. They would not recognise who we have become.

For when we have 'died', we begin to rediscover that we are truly spiritual beings, beings who can take on many forms and exist concurrently in many dimensions. We remember that we can travel through the universe without the aid of vehicles and the temporary, embodied personalities we once used.

When we are leaving this life ourselves, those who have gone before come back to us in a recognisable form to help us with the transition and adjustment we have to make. Often, just prior to death, those about to pass on will mention that they can see their already 'dead' relatives — usually explained away as hallucination or mental collapse. But those images, those beings showing us some of their light from other levels of life, are telling us that we are never alone; we are always helped through to the next level of being. The universe is a place of healing, a true realm of spiritual light and power.

A Prayer for Passing

If you know of someone who is about to pass on from this life to the next, or who has recently done so, pause and think of them for a moment.

Remember that they will gradually loosen their connection with their physical and energy bodies, returning them to the earth from which they came.

Give thanks for their life, and offer this prayer, or a similar one of your own:

> *Divine being, your servant, [their name],*
> *grows now into his/her realm of great light,*
> *embraced by your love and the guiding hands*
> *of the ancestors and loved ones, gone on before.*
> *The angels are with him/her.*
> *Thank you for his/her life, the blessings it has shed on us,*
> *and the perfect journey that he/she now makes.*

In your inner vision, see them moving into their perfect, soul-blessed, golden light.

And let them go.

CHAPTER 7
THE SHINING ONES

*He will put his angels in charge
of you, to guard you;
They will hold you up on their hands
Lest you hurt your foot on a stone.*

Luke 4:10

Heartstar

In Chapter 1, I mentioned the night visitors I met as a boy. Though sometimes they were a little less than friendly, mostly they were quite beautiful and of a kind and loving disposition.

These most beautiful souls, whoever they were, visited me increasingly over the years, usually appearing to me in a beautiful pale blue light and, as part of my understanding of things, they were and still are, very important indeed.

A meeting with another famous clairvoyant, now passed into a higher life, told me of these beings, how they were sent from God to help others. I assumed they were some kind of angel or entity, rather like the splendid and sometimes wonderful guides or great souls, beings no longer embodied but who can help those of us who are here to learn, to grow and to serve.

My relationship with these entities has developed and now they are known to me collectively, and affectionately, as 'Heartstar'. They teach me (and thousands of others) to serve, love and be prepared for the great change now occurring in humanity, both here on the planet and elsewhere in the universe. The words and light of Christ are amplified by them and explained along with fresh, compelling insights. It is all truly wonderful. It also explained to me why as a child I was often transfixed by the stars in a cloudless sky when I looked upward on clear evenings to behold their magnificence, especially that of the Dog Star, Canis Major, or Sirius. As I write these words, a beautiful tingling wave of magic washes over me. Can you remember how you felt when you viewed the Milky Way in your early years, when you looked up and saw the sheer majesty of it all?

Reflection on the stars

If you have forgotten the magic of the stars (most of us tend eventually to take them for granted), find some time to observe them, to appreciate them and maybe even communicate with them.

On a clear night, as far away as possible from the light pollution of our street and urban lights, gaze up at the stars.

Simply behold the majesty revealed in the tapestry of the night sky.

Study the Milky Way in all its magnificence, and see which stars attract you most. There are many simple diagrams available that will help you recognise the stars and constellations.

Listen to the stars. Let them call you. You may, in time, discover connections that surprise you.

A revelation

Tony, a client, came to see me. He had been suffering from the energy-sapping illness diagnosed as M.E. and, as a successful self-employed film-maker and animator, he needed all the energy he could find to survive in a competitive market. He is extremely talented and, during his consultation, we sought ways of helping him sustain his energy levels through healing and visualisation techniques.

On his return home, Tony decided to do some more healing visualisations and suddenly he was confronted by an entity bathed in a beautiful blue light. The entity had come to help him with his healing and spoke of a connection with star system Sirius, evidently its place of origin.

A few days later, a picture arrived for me through the post. Tony had painted his vision and sent the painting to me to see if I understood who this creature shedding the beautiful light on him might be.

My jaw dropped in amazement! Before me was a very close likeness to one of the visitors I first saw as a boy in my North London bedroom. This was one of the Heartstar entities that had seemed to be so close to me, guiding me and helping me. It appeared that they had used the situation to confirm their existence and connection with me. It also explained my fixation with Sirius as a youngster and my connections there. Currently, it is understood in some esoteric circles that Sirius is our twin solar and star system, rather like an older brother, and that our patterns of understanding are largely determined by this relationship (I recommend *The Sirius Mystery* by Robert Temple for more on this idea and its history).

The childhood of a Catholic can have its more destructive aspects, not least the guilt and feelings of undeservedness that are instilled. But one of the positive areas is the encouragement of a mystical awareness, and a belief in intercession from other dimensions and great beings who are no longer physically present on the earth. The Communion of Saints and Martyrs is a recognition of this truth, albeit a rather limited one. It opens the heart to the notion that we are not alone, and all major cultures accept spiritual guidance from ancestors and forbears, as well as sometimes from angels and divine messengers.

For me, the Heartstar connection and my Catholic upbringing now converged and I gained further understanding of what

I had seen and felt all my life. My experiences had always been real to me but Tony's story now confirmed what in my heart I already knew. If any 'proof' of such things is possible — this was a wonderful proof to have!

Angels

I have seen angels in all types of situations, all my life. From the higher angels who help us in moments of great upliftment and devotion, to those elemental, nature devas or spirits who work among the plants and trees and rocks and soil of our planet.

To me, angels are as real as everything else in life. They are the engineers of light, enabling the divine pattern and plan to unfold — from the seraphim who look into the eyes of God and keep reality in place, to the arch angels and guardians who work closely with us, helping us reveal our part of the plan through our lives as effectively and efficiently as possible. The more we pray, meditate and cooperate, the more they can help us and synchronise our lives.

They work through our intuition, our inner voice and inner vision and through the tapestry of our lives and circumstances. They know our soul's message for us and will help us follow it if we so allow.

To my mind, and here I disagree a little with such eminences as Steiner and Swedenborg, angels are a separate kingdom to that of the human, as are flowers and vegetables, animals and minerals. I believe they have never been human in the sense that we have and are not subject to the same choice patterns we experience. The dark or fallen angels (for example, Lucifer) are a part of God's willingness to give us choice and allow us to experience darkness or separation from God's ideal if we choose to for a while. They are engineers, a part of the plan.

But for your entire incarnation, you have a guardian angel who works with you to help and encourage you, giving you 'ears to hear and eyes to see'.

The doctor and his angels

Some of my most vivid and magical encounters with angels have been on visits to southern Germany. One in a centre where I have worked. It belongs to two doctor friends who live near to Munich who have built a large, beautiful pyramid-like structure in which they now run their 'cabinets' or medical practices. There are also some large rooms for meditation and workshops, and these I have used on occasion, especially for teaching purposes.

One weekend I was giving a workshop for some twenty or so people when I noticed the appearance of angelic creatures, one in each corner of the room. They had that distinctive shimmering, almost metallic appearance so distinctive of angels, each had slightly different colouring and was radiating a series of incandescent lights, filling the space between them where the course participants were sitting and working. It was a most beautiful sight, and several of the students also became aware of their presence. I have learned since that these beings come not so much to protect us, but to create and sustain the light and energy frequencies most conducive to the creative work we are seeking to do. They work a little like divine engineers, holding in place the necessary subtle structures that we need, enabling us to work at more exalted levels as effectively as we can.

Later on, I discussed what we had seen with Dr Willy Bornschein, one of the two physicians who owned and worked in the building. He smiled broadly, obviously delighted by what we were reporting to him.

'I always invoke the help of angels as I prescribe for my patients,' he said.

They certainly seemed to know their way around the building!

Remember that, in each human being, there is something of everything that is in the universe — there is something of everything in you, including an angel. The angel of the presence, mentioned in some of the exercises in this book, is the angel of your being, helping you to sustain your life here on earth. You also have a solar or soul angel in you. It is the aspect of your soul or higher self that brings the potentially perfect being in you to take on a human mind and body and human emotions, to live on earth for a lifetime. Through this angel in you, you can contact the other angels — it is your reference point for angelic experience.

Confetti of light

Although I cannot accept much of the limiting doctrinal thinking that often seems to be the way of the church, I still consider myself a Christian, one who loves the message of the Christ, exemplified in the life of Jesus. I can still enjoy the communion of the Mass. And I am often consulted by priests — both Catholic and Protestant.

I try to ensure my children understand the true, central meaning of the Christian message and the liberation it can bring to human beings: 'It's nothing without love, but with love, it's everything.'

We do still attend Mass occasionally. One of my most beautiful memories was at the time of the celebration of the First Holy Communion at my son's school. The energy of children, aspiring, hoping, dreaming and expecting, as it does, always has the power to lift us all and, for me, school services and Masses are especially beautiful and uplifting. The power and clear spiritual light of the children helped me to a wonderful perception at the time of this very special day.

The church was light, bright and full of joyful expectancy. We watched and prayed for all the children there — the energy was tangible, even the most insensitive of individuals would have experienced the odd nerve tingle here and there.

At once, around the altar, the power of four great lights struck me. They shone so brightly, like gold and silver jewels that shimmered and glowed. They were so beautiful, vibrant and alive, revealing the glory of another realm of life, a realm we have all since forgotten, but one that can do so much to help us grow nearer to the magnificent truth of ourselves. This was the light of the angels, a brilliance I had witnessed many times in my life before. They came to support the reaching out in the hearts of those present to touch those innocent and optimistic ideals expressed in the children we love and for whom we have such great dreams and hopes. They also brought with them a beautiful light to help us pray and aspire.

When the service ended, the scene was reminiscent of that I have witnessed on various other occasions. The vibrant light in the church, rising like a great mantle above the congregation, stretching from one end to the other, began to break up just as it does in the human aura as moods change and energies move and readjust. The church appeared to be filled with a glittering, sparkling confetti of silver, gold and other multicoloured lights cascading around everyone's shoulders as we left the building. When we throw confetti, whether rice at weddings, flower petals at religious ceremonies, or even ticker-tape at football matches and political rallies, it respresents symbolically this great light that breaks around individuals at the centre of joyful attention and good feeling. I had often seen this at weddings and on some church and spiritual occasions but never so powerfully and with such clarity as I witnessed on that day.

Just a day or so ago, at a break in one of my workshops, a student who is well known to me spoke of a friend who had recently married and who, at the end of the ceremony, was puzzled yet also a little elated by the sparkling bright lights she could see, apparently falling from nowhere as they cascaded all around her. This had nothing to do with stained-glass windows or any other physical phenomenon. With her consciousness raised by the high emotion of the moment, she attuned to this beautiful light of the higher planes, as it broke around her family. It is truly 'angel dust' and often falls from thought forms as they travel around us.

We are entering an age when we will all see and know far more than we do now and I have yet to see a prediction that even touches the glory of what I feel we will all grow to perceive and understand in the years ahead. Then we will all see, believe, and indeed know so much more than we do at present. Exciting times indeed.

Guardian Angels, Guides and Nature Spirits
Connecting

Exercise 26

1. Relax and breathe deeply. Give thanks for your life on earth and fill yourself with beautiful light and radiate.

2. Focus your attention in your heart chakra and imagine it to be the doorway into a glorious inner garden — a very precious space.

3. Open the door and step through into this most beautiful flower garden, full of blooms, all the colours you can imagine and more besides. Enjoy it for a while, observe, see, feel, smell and hear it all. Use your senses to the full to savour this wonderful space.

4. In your garden, nature is at work perfectly, all the wonderful nature spirits and fairy lights are weaving their magic to sustain this place for you. Serving is their task and their pleasure. Notice how clear and bright the lights of these elementals are. Thank them.

5. Find the peaceful clearing in your garden where you can pause for a while.

   Consider the vast unseen network of help available to you and your world, especially the devic kingdom, that of higher angels, lesser angels and nature spirits. As you rest here, allow yourself to become aware of the angel who is special to you. It is your guardian, with you at all times from before birth until after death.

Your guardian will show you their light if you are patient. It is unmistakable, shimmering and almost metallic, like the angels I used to see around the altar as a boy. The light of your guardian will be unique and you will remember them, when they appear to you, like an old friend, long forgotten. Thank them for being there.

6   Ask your guardian to give your love to your guide, the discarnate entity who exists as a higher mental being to guide you and walk with you in this life. They may not appear to you yet. That will happen when you are ready.

7.   Enjoy your garden and the teeming life within it for a few moments more, then return to the doorway in your heart. Step through into the physical world again and be still for a few moments.

8.   Clear and radiate, connecting well with the earth well before slowly opening your eyes and returning to normal awareness.

Guardians of the woods and mountains

One of my favourite things, when I have time, is to walk through woods and, whenever possible, up the beautiful mountains of Germany, Switzerland and Austria. It is especially magical for me to observe the lights of the lesser angels, the devas and elementals as they work amongst the trees and flowers, rocks and rivers, helping to sustain the ever changing life in this three-dimensional world.

On a recent trip to Switzerland, looking at the breathtaking light near Lake Lucerne as the elementals and the devas toiled away together was like gazing into a cave of a million moving stars of all possible colours. I paused briefly, to take it all in, to let

it penetrate as deeply as possible into my heart. There is nothing
to compare with the sense of belonging, the mystical awareness
of unity and connection that such an encounter awakens in us,
and my mild entrancement somewhat puzzled my Swiss com-
panions, until I explained the reason for my behaviour. They may
have thought I was a bit crazy, but I didn't mind!

The mountains of the Allgau, that beautiful region in the
south of Bavaria, nestling up to its Alpine brothers as Germany,
Austria and Switzerland all converge, are a special treasure to
me, as are the dear friends I have there. My two sons have
accompanied me on several trips and if ever there was a place
filled with magic and the healing power of life, this is certainly
one of them.

I shall never forget my first visit during a beautiful sunny
June, when the rivers ran freely, with the still-melting snow at
the mountain tops providing the fuel for their surge down the
slopes into the valley. My friend, Hansjorg, and his family, took
me many times into 'their valley', the Oytal, near Oberstdorf,
and we climbed the mountains up to the snow-line to behold a
view whose memory has thrilled me again and again since. The
power of the mountains, the permanence and the agelessness
they convey somehow sharply define for me the transient nature
of this worldly human life and our dependence on those greater,
wiser forces of the universe for our growth and sustenance. You
do not have to be religious to have such a spiritual
experience when in the presence of these great solid giants and
the life they support throughout the seasons and cycles of life.

On one particular occasion, the mountain seemed to
breathe, to be alive, and at once my perception shifted until I felt
like a child who was being embraced, hugged by this grand old
being. Around me I could see many wonderful lights as they
sparkled through the trees and across the craggy face of the
mountain — purples, silvers, vivid emeralds and golds, ruby and

copper reds, as the angelic guardians of this wonderful territory revealed themselves to me.

I felt so humble, I remember walking away from my friends a little, falling to my knees and saying, 'Thank you, thank you.'

Now I understand the sacredness of mountains and how they are alive with angels and devas, working the perfect alchemy of these spaces that man will never completely conquer and damage. Like people, mountains too, have guardians.

Contacting your guardian angel

Exercise 27

1. Remember the solar angel, the angel of your soul who is contacted through your heart.
2. Imagine a beautiful golden light glowing and radiating from your heart.
3. Then, think of your guardian angel.

   Take a piece of paper and a pencil and write a little note to it, simply acknowledging its presence in your life and thanking it for its help.
4. Decorate your note using coloured pencils or crayons and then place it beneath your pillow at night, asking your guardian to speak to you in your dreams and to help you to be aware of its working in your daily life. Be patient and it will do both of those things for you and more.
5. Remember how the angel in you, the solar angel, will help you to contact your special angel, your guardian. You will experience it, through your own angelic light, all in good time.

To develop and encourage contact, maintain an honest desire to be the best individual you can be, be observant and look for meaning and remarkable coincidences in your life.

Spend time alone in daily prayer and contemplation, and make a practice of seeking out beauty in all you see and experience.

Be attentive to nature, through your garden, your flowers and trees, in the parks you visit and the wonders of the countryside.

Keep a record of your spiritual journey and all the signals of angelic support and the magic working in your life. The more you seek, the more you will see.

And trust your guardian angel. You will find that your awareness of it and the angelic realm will grow and grow.

Your guide

Sadly, the nature of discarnate guides is often misunderstood. There are many discarnate entities who may appear to be guides. Many guides given to congregations in Spiritualist churches are in fact thought forms, often remnants from old magical practices in earlier cultures of North America, Latin America, Africa and the Far East.

The higher guides, who contact us when we have reached sufficient maturity, are there to be a reference point for us, because they understand the physical life, our destiny and have a broader view of life than we tend to while we are on earth.

They are not there to dictate the pattern of our lives for us, or to take responsibility for us, making our decisions. No evolved being at any level of life would take your power away from you in that way. The guides are there to help us make our own decisions, to walk with us and to teach us, and, in exceptional circumstances, to teach and heal through us.

My own guide, Heartstar, comes to teach and heal through me sometimes and it has taken me many, many years to establish that contact and to develop it to the level it is now, where through me Heartstar teaches many people all over the world.

Initially, we should seek to give our guides opportunity to contact us using a similar approach to that we use with our guardian angel:

~ Acknowledge their presence and thank them for it.
~ Ask them for help and guidance that you may follow your destiny and your plan on earth, for only in such a way can you be truly happy, joyful and fulfilled.
~ Each week, put a little time aside to allow your guide to come close to you.

Exercise 28

1. Make a sacred space for your ritual.

   Rituals are good for us in any higher, spiritual activity, whether contacting guides, angels or linking with our souls through prayer and meditation. If possible, have a few fresh flowers in the room, light a beautiful candle and generally bless the space around you as you prepare. Also, use music to create a light, joyful ambience.

2. Offer a little prayer of dedication:

   I offer my life to service and to following my true path.
   I invite the higher guides who will help me and guide me on
   my way, to be with me and show to me how God's light,
   love and wisdom can express through me and my life.

   Such a prayer creates beautiful light around you and opens the door in your heart and mind to higher guidance.

3. Briefly follow the clearing and radiating exercise.

4. Sit in the stillness of your room in silent meditation, focusing on your heart chakra. Imagine your heart to be like a beautiful rose, a symbol for Divine Love.

5. As the image or idea of the rose becomes stronger, be aware of the beautiful loving guidance that is available to you, especially through your guides, at all times. It comes from their heart to your heart. Welcome that guidance, however and whenever it may come to you.

6. Sit in the stillness for a while longer and, when you feel ready

(and you will know when that is), return to normal consciousness, clearing, radiating and grounding as you usually do.

In the afterglow of the experience, you may be inspired to make some notes, write a verse, a poem, or draw a picture. If you are musical, you may feel inspired to sing, play, or dance, so keep the creative tools you may need close by during these sessions.

Don't be disappointed if nothing much seems to happen early on. You are seeking to develop a relationship and any such thing takes time and patience. Be regular and committed in your practice. In my early working years, I used the same time and day every week, without fail, until the contact was well established. Then I was able to become more flexible.

Try to avoid some of the usual pitfalls with this area of spiritual life. The two most common are becoming obsessed by the idea so you include the guides in every sentence of every conversation and refusing to take any personal actions or decisions without their approval. I knew one medium who would not choose a colour or style of clothes in case they were 'not what the guides wanted', and other dear people lay every piece of guidance in their lives at the feet of the discarnate guides, even when choosing a birthday card! To me, this is nonsense. The guides are there to teach us how to make sound choices and judgements regarding our destiny, not to make the judgements for us. And they certainly don't mind what clothes we wear.

Also, continually referring to your guides can be irksome to others. A very important aspect of the relationship is the intimacy between you and your guides. Later, in the right circumstances, you may share your knowledge with others. You have no need to be ashamed of your experiences but, as with all meaningful developments in your life, sometimes it is best, at least at first, to be circumspect and quietly enthusiastic.

Always remember the most important relationship is that between you and your soul, your spiritual self, and it is from there that the central forces and guidance for your life emanate.

Let the relationship unfold naturally, slowly and gently and it will enrich your life.

And do not compare your experience to that of others, except from a research and understanding point of view. My own experience has told me that the great diversity of the universe is reflected in all dimensions of its nature, and no two manifestations of anything can or should be exactly the same. Allow your unfoldment to be creative and natural, your own. At my workshops, I tell people to 'think snowflake' — we are all similar, yet different!

Bad Spirits

Many people, especially some who are of orthodox religious background, question or even forbid an association with discarnate spirits, mediums or anything to do with the afterlife.

This is both naïve and hypocritical. As a boy, I was encouraged to pray to saints who were a type of 'approved' discarnate, but not to anyone else in case I contacted something evil. We should not touch the occult, or hidden, we are told, in case we meet something nasty or unpleasant that will take over and control us in some way. Yet we meet difficult, unpleasant and even evil people throughout our lives. Why is it acceptable to take such an apparent risk in our earthly lives and not in another?

Frankly, such negative attitudes are driven by fear and ignorance. I have seen and conversed with these discarnates all my life and I am neither evil, stupid, obsessed nor controlled in any way. While I am human and may have my faults, my essential motivation is to do good and loving things and help people heal themselves and their lives.

Any work in this field does not require the suspension of common sense and good moral judgement. No guide of any evolution would ask of you anything that went against your own high values. 'My guide told me to do it,' is no excuse for destructive, harmful or imprudent words or actions.

The good sound practice advocated in these pages, accompanied by pure, high motivation (for our motives truly reveal who we are) is all that we need. Certainly the sensation seeker, the egotist, or the cruel, will attract like-minded souls both on this plane and others — that is the nature of things, the divine law, the laws of attraction. But those that seek wisdom, pure magic, enlightenment, and to better themselves and consequently their contribution to life, have nothing at all to fear.

And always keep your sense of humour. My own guides, as with all higher guides, have a wonderful and gentle sense of fun, and laughter frequently ripples around my workshops, especially when they are involved directly. I too have a great sense of fun and could not easily survive without it on my busy schedule. Humour dissipates negativity at all levels of life.

Possession

I have often been asked to look at cases where there is the suspected control of individuals by earthbound spirits. This kind of possession is in fact extremely rare and I have seen only one really genuine case in all those I have investigated over the years.

It was in a highly intelligent man who had bought a small Buddhist shrine from an antique shop in Hong Kong and ever since had felt dominated by a discarnate Japanese monk. Attempts at meditation and healing were always intruded upon by this entity, who would become very angry and aggressive in his attempts to manage and retain possession over this man's psyche. However, when I was helping in the healing and clearing of the entity, I was aware that the man did not truly wish to release the old monk's intrusions and even in his fear there was a perverse enjoyment.

Using the practices of this book, such things will not happen to you. You will not meet evil spirits unless you want to.

Earthbound Souls

We are beings of many levels. Your soul is your individual spiritual nature or higher self and it cannot be earthbound, or trapped in a three-dimensional sense.

What can and sometimes does happen is that some remnants of a personality persisting after physical death may connect to locations on the earth that were significant to them, as we saw in Chapter 6. Usually, the link is due to some powerful emotional activity, possibly extreme shock and sadness or great joy or affection.

At our local airfield, which was a main USAF base in World War Two for Flying Fortress B17s, there is a control tower and it became apparent that many entities were still attached to it. In other words, fragments of their personalities still 'visited' the site. Even those not especially clairvoyant or psychically sensitive could detect an unusual, busy and very cool atmosphere in the place. I was able to see evidence of many entities, especially from wartime, linked to the place; mostly it was a gentle connection. The presence of girls who had worked in the telegraph and operations office, one or two young airmen and the caretaker who had supervised and lived in the building after the war, were quite vivid and active, and generally quite pleasant.

However, there was one entity, initially detected by my wife, who was very unhappy. He had been a young airman who could not cope with the awful losses of life he had witnessed in that time, and part of his being (essentially his lower astral nature) was still linked to the emotional pull of those experiences. He was still living a little in that part of himself, in the emotional or

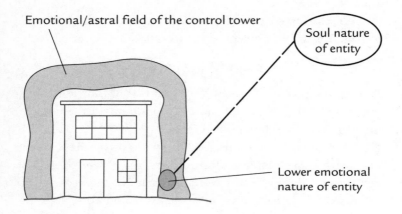

Figure 19 An entity still linked with the physical realm through the emotional plane.

astral field of the control tower and the thought forms and memories it held within it (see Figure 19).

And while this didn't actually make his soul earthbound, it seemed to act as an inhibitor on the other activities of the soul and its other bodies or selves. This entity was still reliving some of its old wartime experiences through its emotional or astral body.

We conducted a beautiful ceremony in the tower, with some healing activities and blessings, and the tower is now much clearer, the entity's presence not evident anymore. It has let go of its past, as we should all do. When our thoughts and feelings are held too firmly in the past, especially by sad or destructive experiences, we leave some of our energy or power behind us in that time and space until we have completely let go.

If you ever have such an experience, though they are not that common, do involve an experienced healer and clairvoyant, familiar with such situations, so that a happy and simple clearing can take place. Locally, both the police and the Citizens Advice Bureau have my telephone number and occasionally refer people to me for help. You should always make similar enquiries in such circumstances.

From Other Planes

Some of the revelations and discoveries in my life have been a little challenging for me, particularly when I discovered that I could act as a channel for many things from other subtle levels of life.

Among these was my capacity to go into what is usually deemed an 'altered state of consciousness', or trance, and to allow Heartstar to come to teach and help others. This trusting relationship was developed over many years until, in given circumstances, I could enable them to talk directly through me to others. I found the trance state relatively easy to attain. And, though some may feel that this is rather like handing myself over recklessly to other beings who might not have my own or others' best interests at heart, I have learned to trust Heartstar and in this approach to spiritual connection which is as old as man himself.

It is, in effect, a sharing of minds with our ancestors who have gone before us and whose place in the universe is more elevated and developed than our own. All religions have benefited from prophets, wise men and teachers who could do such things and, while I do not consider myself to be either prophet or wise man, it is my role to teach. And I have learned above all else is that there are two profound universal laws we should always apply when making our assessments and decisions.

The first is the principle of magnetisation and attraction. The human being is rather like a magnet. We attract to ourselves that which we both are and that which we need, and the law of attraction governs in this process. If we are evil, we tend to attract evil until we wake up to the truth about ourselves, change our thinking and so alter our magnetism. 'As a man thinketh in his heart, so is he!' But we will also attract those who can help us grow and change, whatever our tendencies at the time. My relationship with Heartstar works on this principle and, while I am certainly not yet perfect myself, my motivation in my work is sincere.

The second principle is 'By their fruits shall ye know them.' These days, or perhaps it has always been so, in esoteric and spiritual circles, there are many people following delusions. They make grand claims as to who they are and what great being they are connected to from another level. But names and status have rarely impressed me. And my love of the work of Jesus, the Christ, is based on its earnest honesty, accessibility and simplicity. Today, spiritual teaching is often highly complicated and full of jargon and hypothesis; I have even seen the soul body reduced to a series of geometric shapes in one current teaching.

My respect for Heartstar is based on the loving, wise and healing nature of the guidance they give, and the freedom to live the good creative lives they encourage in us. I am honoured to be associated with such a beautiful and inspirational source and I am happy to share some of my time with them, both at home and abroad, that they may help others.

Currently, many 'channels' suggest that their contacts are not from earth but from other planets or stars. Heartstar has its own centre around the star system Sirius. But such entities do not visit us in space ships, UFOs or the like (though I am not saying these do not exist as my experience tells me otherwise). Truly evolved beings travel through consciousness and do not need vehicles as we do to move through the universe. In fact, they do not even need planetary homes in the same sense that we do.

However, Heartstar has told me and others on many occasions, it is not who they are, where they come from or how they get here that matters, it is the light they bring that counts.

I trust this book will help and lead you to somewhere new, to a fresh vision or two, or at least to a sense that life is far more than it seems.

Perhaps now, you may recall some of the time before you arrived in this world, the marvellous web of light and life that works with you, largely unseen, all your days. And know that you will never die, merely move on and through to new territories of experience when the time comes.

What a remarkable life you have.

APPENDIX
SOME MEDITATION
EXERCISES

These exercises will help you in the development of your daily meditation, over and above any of the exercises in this book you may choose to explore.

Meditation has one main purpose and is, or at least should be, central to any life. Meditation is true healing and helps us to link our personalities (our body, emotions and mind) to our souls and higher selves and the supreme guidance awaiting us. It produces the perfect magnetism of our souls within our personalities so that we may attract in our lives the most creative circumstances for us to experience.

I always suggest a period of meditation first thing in the morning before eating or any other activity, followed by another later in the day if possible. The duration of meditations may vary but usually between 20 and 30 minutes is enough. Also, because the earth's magnetic pole is shifting very rapidly, it is good to pause briefly throughout the day just for a minute or so to reconnect through your crown chakra to the light of your soul and spirit. These brief links are an extremely useful back up for the main meditational periods and help us to stay balanced and in tune in fast-changing times.

Meditation 1

1. Go through the clearing and radiating exercise.
2. Place your focus around your heart chakra and concentrate three slow, rhythmic breaths through the heart, breathing in through the front of the heart and out through the back.
3. After the third breath, think the words *I AM*. Say them slowly, repeating them occasionally as your thoughts may stray away to other things (the first part of any meditational activity is the acquisition of powers of concentration and thought control).
4. Gradually, allow the words to be said inside your heart. You may be able to visualise this or feel it, or both.
5. Next, slowly guide these words and the sound they make inside you, upwards from your heart.
6. Lead them gradually upwards until they echo inside your head, repeating them slowly and gently as you do. Don't worry if your mind drifts again. Just gently direct your thoughts back to the '*I AM*' and all will be well.
7. After a time (you will know intuitively when), draw the process to a close and into reverse by travelling gently downwards with the '*I AM*' until you feel your focus is around your heart again.
8. Step through your heart, clear and radiate as you do so and then ground yourself.
9. Open your eyes slowly. You are opening your channels beautifully.

It is now time to do your healing prayers, affirmations and constructive visualisations for others and yourself before going about your everyday activities.

This meditation approach is for commencing a deep process of meditation and soul-link. Whilst you will be surrounded by angels and guides in this process as they love you and will help you, it is not a time for a conscious linking with them or for other 'journeys'. This is dealt with in other activities and specific exercises in this book.

Meditation 2

When you feel you have mastered Meditation 1 (usually after a few weeks), progress to this exercise.

1. Clear and radiate.
2. Go through Meditation 1, this time lifting your focus from heart to head a little more directly now. Never rush in any spiritual exercise, but glide up until your concentration is in your head.
3. Concentrate on the space above your eyes, behind your forehead, where the brow chakra is located.
4. Allow the beautiful light there to form slowly.

   this unfoldment takes will vary from individual to individual and meditation to meditation. Be patient. If you persist, the light will form, even if it takes weeks to do so. It will most often appear like a cloud of amethyst-purple light, wispy and thin in its extremities, but increasingly intense the nearer the centre. In the centre, the light will eventually reveal itself to you with a wonderful brilliance, beyond any description I can offer.
5. Breathe slowly and rhythmically three times through the light, or in the stages before the light is clearly visible to you, through the brow chakra or centre — in through the front and out through the back of your head. Enjoy the experience, returning your focus to it gently, yet firmly if your mind should wander to other thoughts.
6. Eventually, return slowly to your heart centre and conclude as in Meditation 1.

When you are experiencing some success with this meditation, go a little more directly to the head and the light at your brow. Practice will make this easier for you. Work at this meditation for several weeks, or maybe a month or more, before progressing to the next.

Appendix

Meditation 3

1. Start with clearing and radiating and go through the stages of Meditations 1 and 2 until your focus is in your head.
2. Look again at the beautiful light at your brow.
3. Then, as if you are gently redirecting the lens of a telescope, you move your attention from your brow slowly upwards until you are looking up at your crown centre.
4. As you do so, be aware you are linking your brow and your crown, the pituitary and pineal glands, your mind and your soul.
5. Breathe in three times through your crown and down along your spine, out through the root centre, and then concentrate on the light of your crown.
6. In time, the most beautiful light will show in your head. Initially it may appear like a ball or disc of white-gold light. As things progress, then a small dot will appear in the centre of the light, getting larger and larger as your meditation develops.
7. Eventually, the light will appear like a golden halo, vibrant and clear. And your head will be full of light.
8. Conclude by retracing your steps as in Meditation 1.

When you have reached this stage, there is nothing for me to add except to encourage you to continue to seek the beautiful light in you and let the wisdom it will bring embrace you.

INDEX

Index

Dr. Bach's Rescue Remedy, 44, 46, 94
dreams, night-time, 10–12, 83, 169–71
drug addiction, 42–3
dying, 21, 177
  helping the, 54–7
  and souls, 166–7

earthbound souls, 195–7
earth's aura, 34, 159–60, 159–62
earth's ley lines, 149–54
Einstein, Albert, 51
Ellison, Arthur, 165
emotional and mental planes, visions of, 10, 41–4
emotional (astral) body, 18–20, 31–5
emotionally centered people, 167
emotional quality of visions, 4–5
emotional ties and cords, 79, 128–31
emotions, importance of, 4–5
emotions, negative, 67
energising particles, 20–21
energy-based healing methods, 25–6
energy centers. see chakras
enterprise, energistics of, 140–49
  and owners, 145–7
  patterns and cycles in, 147–9
epilepsy, 5–6
etheric doubles, 24–5
etheric (energy) body, 20–24, 125
  after death, 172–5
euthanasia, 166
evil spirits, 193–5, 197–8
exercises
  attunement exercises and closing down, 29–30
  for attuning to rays of one's own aura, 88–9
  auric awareness, 34–5
  to clear and radiate energy, 28
  clearing the chakras, 99–101
  connecting with colours, 58–9

connecting with guides, guardians and nature spirits, 186–7, 189–92
to connect with earth's aura, 161–2
to connect with intuitive flow, 121–3
to connect with unfolding destiny, 119–20
to consider those in the afterlife, 168–9
for dissipating anger, 120–21
for hand-sensing of chakras, 123–6
for healing and bringing light, 44–5
for ley-spotting outdoors, 156
for ley-spotting with maps, 154–5
for perceiving colours of someone's auric field, 89–91
for release from cording, 130–31
to stimulate etheric vision, 26–7
to test aura of object, 139–40
for thought form perception, 39–40
to tune into aura of buildings, 137–8
to tune into aura of your locality, 136–7
to tune into the energy field of seeds, 158–9

fairies, citing of, 7–8, 158
famous people's auric colours, 63
fatigue, overcoming, 22–3
fear, effects of, 52, 130, 175, 193 93–4
flowers, 27, 34, 157–8
food and visions, 9–10
force absorption, process of, 102, 103
forgiveness, practice of, 130–31

Gaia awareness, 159
ghosts, 172–5
God, love of, 78

Index

prayers, 25, 36, 66, 77, 139, 169
  and aspiration, 41
  for passing life, 178
pre-birth experiences, memory of,
  48–9, 92, 177, 199
products, aura of, 147
promiscuity, effects of, 73, 129–30
psychic centres. *see* chakras, 23
psychics
  extent of powers of, 55, 104, 142
  misinformation from, 30, 32, 52,
    76–7, 101–2, 165, 176, 198
psychometry, 48, 137, 139–40

radionics, 25
reflections and colour consciousness,
  63–4
relationship problems, 73, 75–6,
  129–30
resentment, effects of, 33
'riding' a business, 146
rituals, 191–2
Rod of Caduceus, 127, 152

second sight, 61
seeds aura of, 128–9
self-development, 120–23
services, aura of, 147
sexual energy, 73, 74–5, 129–30
singing, 17, 24
sleeping, 169–71
smells, 13
solar plexus chakra, 9–10, 23,
  28, 33, 34, 111
  cords, 219
  and dying, 166, 167
  healing, 44
solar system's aura, 34, 159–62
soul angel, 184
soul lights and babies, 48–9

souls, 25, 54, 118
  and dying, 167
  earthbound, 195–7
  your relationship with your, 193
spirits, 176–7
stars, 180, 181
Steiner, Dr. Rudolph, 159
storms, 12–14
strokes, 168
subconscious, the, 29–30, 32, 47, 49
sun's aura, 20, 96, 159–62

Tae Kwon Do, 74
Temple, Robert, 181
thought forms, 36–9, 40, 175–6,
  177, 186
tissue regeneration, 24
towns, chakras of, 132–7
trances, 197–9
trees, aura of, 27, 157–8
troubled people, healing for, 44–5

understanding the world, 16, ix–x
universal mental energy, 78–9

visions. *see* childhood visions
visual dictionary or reference chart,
  keeping a, 40

water, aura of, 156–7
Watkins, Alfred, 149
woods, guardians of, 187–8
Wordsworth, William, 16
world, understanding of, 16, ix–x

yoga, 74

AUTHOR'S DETAILS

Paul Lambillion has a range of self-help and teaching cassettes and flower colour essences which are available by mail order. He also gives seminars and workshops in the UK and overseas. Full details and information on all aspects of Paul's work may be found at
www.paullambillion.dial.pipex.com
and *www.heartwayusa.com*
or you can email him direct at
paullambillion@dial.pipex.com.